SURVIVING HELL

NICK DUNN

MIRROR BOOKS

...published by Mirror Books in 2020

Mirror Books is part of Reach plc
10 Lower Thames Street
London EC3R 6EN

www.mirrorbooks.co.uk

ISBN 978-1-912624-86-7

Typeset by Danny Lyle

Printed and bound in Great Britain by
CPI Group (UK) Ltd, Croydon, CR0 4YY

A CIP catalogue record for this book is available from the British Library.

Every effort has been made to fulfil requirements with regard to
reproducing copyright material. The author and publisher will be
glad to rectify any omissions at the earliest opportunity.

1 3 5 7 9 10 8 6 4 2

Cover images: iStockphoto / Barry Marsden

This book is dedicated to my incredible sister,
Lisa Dunn, and to my amazing mam, Margaret Dunn,
with my love and gratitude for keeping me going when
I thought there was no hope left.

CONTENTS

FOREWORD

Nick Dunn, a man I have come to know well, embodies everything that is exemplary about the British military – or former British soldiers, as Nick was when subjected to a nightmarish ordeal almost beyond compare, as told in these pages.

Let's be clear: Nick Dunn, and the former soldiers arrested alongside him, were utterly innocent of any crime. Innocent. Utterly. Not guilty. No crime committed. Not anywhere.

But let's start at the beginning. Make no mistake, Nick, former 1 PARA and Special Forces Support Group (SFSG), had as fine a story to tell in a book as any man, long before he and his comrades were seized off Indian waters and subjected to four years in hell, slammed behind bars in the baking hot, rat-infested, corrupt and vicious prison system that appears to be the norm in modern-day India.

As an elite soldier, Nick had served in some of the world's worst trouble-spots, including Northern Ireland, Iraq and Afghanistan, cheating death on more than one occasion and being lucky to walk away alive.

Not content with side-stepping the Grim Reaper repeatedly during his time in the military, Nick sought fresh challenges, as the men of the Parachute Regiment – those who wear the maroon beret – are wont to do. He moved into private security work, fighting Somali pirates on the high seas, as he and his fellow private security operators escorted merchant vessels through the world's most dangerous shipping lanes.

It was during one such mission that the Indian coastguard chose to pounce. It was 12 October 2013 when they seized the MV Seaman Guard Ohio, the merchant ship that Nick and crew had been contracted to safeguard from piracy, claiming she had been steaming into Indian waters illegally, and accusing Nick and his fellow operators of carrying illegal weapons into Indian territory, intent on causing untold mischief and mayhem.

So began the descent into hell.

Nick was 27 years old. Hustled into Puzhal Central Prison, in Chennai, capital of the Indian State of Tamil Nadu, the Indian authorities pretty much locked up Nick and his fellows and threw away the key. It wasn't until eighteen months later that the finally got to read the 2,158-page charge sheet, accusing them of their heinous – and wholly fictitious – crimes.

With Nick facing trial, his family raised a petition to free the 'Chennai Six,' as he and his fellow British captives had become known, garnering thousands of signatures.

Languishing in unimaginably horrific conditions, Nick and his fellows were locked into crowded, rat-infested cells, deprived of anything to sleep on, clear water, proper food, and in temperatures soaring above forty-degrees. Rubbing shoulders with murderers, extortionists and rapists, the Chennai Six had been branded as 'terrorists', intent on doing the Indian nation harm. They faced daily abuse – verbal and physical – at the hands of their fellow inmates.

At one stage there was a mass brawl, as Nick and his mates were forced to use their tier-one military training to fight for their very lives. Yet throughout all, Nick Dunn remained bloodied but unbowed.

With Nick facing trial, his sister, Lisa, a tireless campaigner for the release of the Chennai Six, decided to complete the Great North Run in support of the captives, while Nick ran a simultaneous thirteen-mile race himself, doing laps of his prison cell, in support of her.

Fellow inmates looked on, bewildered, believing that Nick had finally cracked. Far from it. Nick was determined that no matter what, he would endure and he would overcome. And amazingly, despite numerous dark and soul-searing low-points, Nick Dunn and his fellow captives remained unbroken by all. Incredible. Extraordinary. So inspiring.

When I first met Nick, he had with him a copy of one of my own books, *SAS Ghost Patrol*. It appeared to be very dog-eared and well-read, which is just what I like to see! I was curious as to why Nick had brought it. He asked me to sign it, explaining that it had been one of the books that he had read during his 49 months rotting in an Indian goal, and that he had used the incredible fortitude and daring of those elite WWII warriors depicted in its pages as inspiration, and to help give him the mental strength to endure.

General Sir David Richards said in his retirement parade, speaking on Horse Guards, in London: 'If I have seen further than most, it was because I stood on the shoulders of giants.' Those men who have served in our elite forces – the Royal Marines, the Parachute Regiment and our Special Forces - are able to do just that, drawing upon the incredible record and exploits of those who founded Britain's elite forces, in the heat and the fire of WWII. Nick Dunn embodies such spirit absolutely.

I was touched by Nick bringing me that book, but hardly entirely surprised. I have met men like Nick in my time both as a war reporter and an author. And more often than not, they embody a set of qualities and an outlook on life – an esprit de corps – that can be best summed up in the Parachute Regiment's own motto: *Utrinque Paritas – ready for anything.*

Nick's courage, his fortitude and his unbreakable spirit reminded me of a poem, Invictus, by William Ernest Henley, and which, because it so utterly embodies the spirit of resistance depicted in the pages of this book, I'd like to quote in full here.

Out of the night that covers me,
Black as the pit from pole to pole,
I thank whatever gods may be
For my unconquerable soul.

In the fell clutch of circumstance
I have not winced nor cried aloud.
Under the bludgeonings of chance
My head is bloody, but unbowed.

Beyond this place of wrath and tears

Looms but the Horror of the shade,

And yet the menace of the years

Finds and shall find me unafraid.

It matters not how strait the gate,

How charged with punishments the scroll,

I am the master of my fate,

I am the captain of my soul.

Those emotive words typify the unbreakable spirit of Nick Dunn – of all the Chennai Six – as depicted in these pages.

I commend this book to you, for it is a truly remarkable and brave story of a truly remarkable man – and a group of men – who refused to buckle or to break, under what to many would have seemed unendurable.

It is also, needless to say, a right riveting read.

Damien Lewis, FRGS, author of *SAS Shadow Raiders*.

CHAPTER 1

NIGHTMARE

Tuticorin District Principal Sessions Court, India
11th January 2016

How could this be happening? And how could it be happening to me? That's what I kept asking myself as this nightmare dragged on. I'm Nick Dunn, one of the Chennai Six. You've probably heard of us. We were British nationals banged up abroad because we were in the wrong place at the wrong time. As former soldiers, we were hired to protect shipping from modern-day pirates, but we were classed as mercenaries and treated like gun runners. We were not only innocent of any crime, there was no crime.

From day one, the authorities in India had decided we were guilty, and that was that. They repeatedly ignored or overruled evidence proving our innocence. We were trapped in a third world country with a shockingly corrupt legal system and used as pawns by those who were out to make a name for themselves. What happened to us was a scandal, and news of our harsh treatment spread around the world.

Before this fateful day – 11 January 2016 – we had already spent more than two years either in jail or on bail, forbidden to leave the country while the case dragged on and on. Now here we were, back in front of a judge for a final resolution.

I had been forced to scrape by, living off handouts from friends and family, army charities, and some of the many well-wishers from the UK who had been following our case in a state of constant astonishment. They were left wondering how we could be treated so poorly by a supposedly friendly nation in the 21st century. The conditions during our extended, forced stay in Chennai – the capital city of Tamil Nadu and formerly known as Madras – were appalling. The heat didn't help. It was one of the hottest places in India where temperatures could regularly reach 35C or even higher.

We were finally about to have our day in court following a trial that had lasted four long months. At last, the judge was going to give his verdict. Surely, common sense and justice would win out, and we would be released. After all, we had done nothing wrong. Anyone with any sense could see that, couldn't they?

I wasn't so sure. My experience up till now had led me to believe anything was possible in India. That was particularly true of Tamil Nadu, the worst state in the country, where we had been imprisoned. The level of corruption was unbelievable. I had seen it all at first hand and experienced the snail's pace at which a case like ours could progress.

As I walked into the court that morning, I was almost late for the verdict thanks to the demands of reporters who were all desperate to get a few words from one of the infamous Chennai Six. They wanted to know how I was feeling and whether I thought our ordeal would soon be over. I was amazed by how many people had been following our story and, if nothing else, that gave me cause for optimism. There was a huge groundswell of support for our release. I told the reporters I was hopeful we might finally get justice, but I was under no illusions.

I might have been a little delayed, but I wasn't going to give my persecutors the satisfaction of letting them see me run, sweating, into court. Instead, I walked in with my head held high. I was experiencing a combination of nerves and excitement at the prospect of finally being released – along with a nagging dread that this still might not go our way.

Back at home in Ashington, 15 miles north of Newcastle, my sister Lisa, who had campaigned tirelessly for our release, was waiting for my phone call to let her know if we would be freed. My mam, who was in very poor health, and my dad were standing by too, both fretting about the outcome. My family had suffered. Their lives had been put on hold, their days filled with worry for me while I was banged up in a notorious, third world prison, full of murderers and rapists. I might not have done anything to deserve my imprisonment, but that didn't stop the guilt I felt for the damage my ordeal was inflicting on my family. I knew I had to get out of here, for them as much as for me, and I had to do it quickly. I prayed it would be today.

I stood at the back of the court room behind a wooden railing and alongside the men who had become my makeshift, dysfunctional family. We faced the judge, the one man with the power to end this nightmare, if only he could show us some mercy. The judge was in his 60s. He was slouched in his chair and peered at us through his glasses, his receding hair partially covered by his ceremonial wig. He looked totally uninterested in us or the case.

There was no jury, so what happened now was entirely down to him. In total, the Indian authorities had arrested and detained 35 men from our ship, including 12 crew and 23 former servicemen. We were on board to guard vessels from attack by notorious Somali pirates. These seaborne raiders had been making worldwide headlines – and a lot of money – storming ships, taking crews prisoner at gunpoint, then ransoming everyone and everything back to their owners and employers, sometimes for millions of dollars.

In the dock with me were 14 Estonians, three Ukrainians and 12 Indians. The rest were from the UK. Us Brits had become widely known as the Chennai Six. Our stories had been written about extensively, not just in the UK but all over the world. Nicholas Simpson was from Catterick; Paul Towers, Pocklington in East Yorkshire; Billy Irving came from Connel in Argyll; Ray Tindall from Chester; and John Armstrong was a Wigton man from Cumbria. We were thrown together as part of the security force on the MV Seaman Guard Ohio and, for better or worse, we were all in this together. The outcome, good or bad, would be the same for us all.

From where we were standing at the back of the court, we couldn't follow the proceedings because the lawyers from both sides had their backs to us and were facing the judge. But, even if we could have heard what was being said, it would have meant nothing. Every word spoken in that court was in Tamil, and none of it translated for our benefit. It was a farce. They were discussing among themselves whether we were innocent or guilty and what should happen to us. Our lives were in their hands, but we couldn't understand a bloody word of it.

The temperature was over 30C that day and we weren't even allowed to sit down. Instead, we stood for hours, all day if that was necessary, while the lawyers argued, and the uninterested judge supposedly deliberated. I don't remember there being fans on the ceiling but, if there were any, they were as much use as tits on a fish for all the good they did.

We were all sweating. The arseholes had even tried to take my bottle of water from me. I told them where to go. I needed something to fight the dehydration.

Ahead of us was a room full of tables and chairs, with the defence team to our right and the prosecution on our left. The judge was on his raised platform, dressed in his robes, his minions around him. A stenographer was taking notes of everything that was said. The Indian legal system was based on the British model, but no reporters were allowed in the court room, and there were no friends or relatives of the accused in the public gallery. The only friendly faces inside the court were a couple of lasses from the British Consulate, Sharon D'Sylva and Manisha Hariharan. They were doing their best to help us because they knew we had done nothing wrong.

Compare our predicament to TV programmes like Banged Up Abroad, which tell the stories of young people who have committed crimes on foreign territories, many involving drugs. These people were often handed down long prison sentences and ended up filled with regret and bitterness because of their stupidity. Their one consolation was their guilt. They deserved their punishment, and they knew it. I hadn't done anything. I didn't deserve this.

The police and prosecution had said the ship we were on board, the MV Seaman Guard Ohio, was trespassing in Indian territorial waters when it was intercepted. It wasn't. Our ship had been moved towards the east coast to meet up with smaller boats supplying us with fuel, and to avoid the aftermath of Cyclone Phailin. Under maritime law, such an act of self-protection was permitted, particularly when there was no intention of heading into port. The coastguards lacked the equipment to pinpoint our actual position and, in court, they were never able to state accurately where we were.

The police also said that six of the weapons we were carrying weren't licensed. They were – and we had the certification to prove it. They doubled down on the claim by calling them illegal, automatic rifles, capable of rapid fire. Our ballistics expert proved in court the police were just plain wrong. Our expert told the judge that these half-dozen Heckler and Koch G3 battle rifles had been adapted to prevent them from ever firing as automatics. The judge said this key evidence had been duly noted, and we hoped that would be enough to secure an acquittal. Our lawyers were from the firm of Anand, Samy & Dhruva, and our defence team was led by a Mr Muthusamy. I never did catch his first name but, like the rest of our small team of lawyers, he was optimistic. Our lawyers told me they had done everything they could, the trial had gone well, and they were convinced everything was looking good.

I don't know how many hours we were standing behind the rail that day waiting for the case to come to a conclusion. Outside it was growing dark. Eventually, the arguing between both sets of lawyers came to a halt, there was a recess for lunch, and we were left to dwell on our fate. An hour later, we were called back into court to hear the verdict from the judge.

Our first suspicion that the ruling had not gone our way came when extra police poured into the courtroom. More than 30 uniformed officers filed in and took up stations around us, blocking all the exits. I remember thinking, if they thought we'd be happy with the verdict, why would they send in reinforcements?

The judge made his final pronouncement in Tamil. We were none the wiser. People started drifting away from the court and we still didn't know our fate. It was ridiculous. One of our lawyers approached. The look on his face told me something was very wrong, and I started to get a very bad feeling. I'm a former Para who has been in combat in two war zones and narrowly avoided death, but I have never seen a man look as terrified as he did in that moment. He was approaching a group of very big guys with very bad news, and we could tell he wanted to be anywhere else but here.

We were all desperate to know what had happened. When we did finally hear the verdict, we were left reeling. "Gentlemen, it is not a good decision," he said. "They have sentenced you to five years' imprisonment on weapons charges."

Eh? What? You're fucking joking? I was stunned. The news hit me like a blow. All the guys around me took the verdict the same way. They looked like I felt. Appalled and disbelieving. Despite our pessimism throughout, we had all still hoped that the Indian court might finally want justice to be done. Instead, this. Five long years.

I felt sick. In the seconds that followed, I began to absorb the terrible reality of my situation. Despite everything we had been told, I was not going to be freed. After six months in jail, followed by more than a year without even being charged, I was about to be put behind bars for a crime I did not commit. And five years! This wasn't just a slap on the wrists from an Indian state looking to teach some foreigners a quick lesson. No, this was long, hard prison time in a hell-hole. Five years!

At that point, I couldn't take in any more. It was too much. I had forced myself to keep going all this time because I had always hoped and believed that, one day, the people in charge of this crazy legal system would finally see sense and we would be released. Now those hopes had been cruelly crushed and, in that moment, I had no idea how I would find the strength to carry on.

One thing I did know – my nightmare was very far from over. It was only just beginning.

LISA'S STORY

That morning, while my brother was waiting to hear the verdict, I was at home in Ashington and about to head over to my mam's house. A close friend of our family, Sheila Davison, was already there, helping my mam to get ready. I was glad of her help because I didn't know exactly when we would get the call from my brother to let us know if he had been freed. That was all I could think about.

I was 34 when Nick was arrested, and all our lives seemed to stop at that point. From that moment, my worry for him was always at the forefront of my mind. Friends told me I should have just got on with my life, but how could I when I knew the hell he was going through? I had seen the awful conditions with my own eyes. I had visited Nick in India and witnessed the way he was forced to live in a third world prison, using a bucket to wash his clothes and himself. He lost a stack of weight because the food was awful and in short supply. I had witnessed an inmate taking a beating from prison guards, and I had seen blood on the floor when another was stabbed. These weren't things I could clear out of my mind and forget. The worry never ended, and I hadn't slept properly in more than two years.

It all came down to this day. We were hopeful of an acquittal. That wouldn't make up for the time Nick had lost, but at least he would be home. We would have my brother back, and we could help him rebuild his life.

The call I had been waiting for finally came. I grabbed the phone. When I heard Nick's voice, I was hoping for the best. He would be released. He might even know the exact time he was coming home. Instead he said, "I'm sorry. We got five years."

I couldn't believe it. I was so shocked. My legs almost buckled. I just kept saying, "no, no, no," over and over again. How could a judge pronounce them guilty when none of the men had done anything wrong? It was barbaric and inhuman.

I went straight over to my mam's house. Nick was on the speakerphone. His voice was filled with emotion, shaky and croaky. But Mam sensed what had happened before he said a word. She could tell by the devastated look on my face. Mam knew it was bad. She started to shake and cry before Nick could even confirm the worst.

When Nick told mam he had been found guilty and had received a sentence of five years, she let out a scream like a wounded animal. She just screamed and screamed. I will never forget the sound of those screams.

CHAPTER 2

BANGED UP

The journey from the court to Chennai prison was 335 miles and lasted a gruelling 14 hours. Because the police insisted there had to be at least one guard for every prisoner under transport, 70 of us were crammed into a bus that was built for half that number. The journey was hair-raising. The driver was crazy and didn't seem to care how fast he was going, or how recklessly he was driving. I constantly expected him to crash.

The ancient rifles carried by our guards were a more pressing threat. As well as old, they were in a bad state of repair, and the men who were supposed to be guarding us kept falling asleep, leaving the barrels waving loosely in the air. My guard's Enfield rifle was uncomfortably close to my face already and, when he dozed off, he slid down, making the danger of a fatal mishap very real. I repeatedly had to push his rifle out of my face. I spent 14 hours thinking he might blow my head off because he kept napping and the road was bumpy. At this rate there was no way all of us were going to make it to prison alive.

My fears about the bus were realised as the driver suddenly lost control of the wheel and the packed vehicle slid across the road then off the edge. We all imagined the worst – and how we didn't end up in a pile of twisted wreckage, I will never know.

The bus had suffered a blow-out. A tyre had burst but, somehow, we hadn't all died in a heap of metal. If that bus had ended up completely off the road, or even upside down, that would have been the end for me. Or maybe I would have suffered only minor injuries. In which case I would have bolted, even if they tried to shoot me. I would have taken my chances on the run, no matter what the odds.

Instead, everyone was shaken but OK and, after a delay, the tyre was replaced. We were on our way again, and we finally arrived at Chennai the next morning, hours later than planned. It had been a hellish long day, and I had been awake for nearly 24 hours. I had tried to sleep on the bus, but it was cramped and hot, and I didn't trust that sleepy guard next to me, with his loaded gun so close to my face.

The reality of our plight was really hammered home when I stepped off that bus. We had been held in this very same prison complex while we were on remand, so we knew exactly how hellish the place could be. This shit was real. There was no avoiding it. Emotions were running high, and all I had echoing around my head was the anguished cry of my mam screaming down the phone when she heard our sentence.

We were led into the prison, our home for the next five years. I was issued with two sheets – nothing else, no pillow or blankets – then led into a cell that had no beds, or even a mattress, to sleep on, just a cold, hard floor. It was grim, but I decided then and there to stay positive. In the Paras, we were trained to assess and deal with any situation. I knew I would need to use all my skills and resilience to survive here. I started that process by choosing a spot to sleep, putting two sheets down to mark the place. I used my trainers and some of my clothes as a pillow and made the best of it.

We were imprisoned with Indian nationals this time. There was no segregation of foreigners as there had been on remand. Now we were convicted, we would be living with the general population. Because we were a big group of westerners, the prison authorities decided to keep us together in a large cell. They crammed all 23 of us in there, including the six Brits and all the Estonian and Ukrainian lads. There were cells nearby that were a lot worse, with up to 40 Indian guys squeezed in together. Still, we were big bulky blokes and took up more room, so we easily filled up the available space.

Not everyone had the same outlook I did, and I don't judge or blame anyone for that. I knew better than most the mindset I needed to adopt if I was going to make it through this nightmare. It was incredibly hard to stay positive when we knew we were innocent and we were facing a long sentence in conditions that would have caused a riot in a British prison, but I was determined to make it through to the bitter end.

My memories of those first days are vivid. I was used to harsh conditions from my time in the Paras, but even I thought the prison was appalling. The toilet was a hole in the ground, there were no showers, and we had to use a big bucket to wash ourselves and our clothes. I had no mattress, so I had to carry on sleeping on a hard, concrete floor.

Over the next few days it began to sink in. These were the conditions we would have to cope with for five years. All our hopes had gone, and we wouldn't be going anywhere in a hurry.

CHAPTER 3

HOW DID I GET HERE?

How did a lad from Ashington end up in a prison in Chennai? The journey from one place to the other was long, slow and often painful. What kind of crazy decisions had I made that saw me leave the north east of England to better myself, only to wind up 5,000 miles away in an Indian jail? Did I end up here because of fate, my own crap judgment, or was it just plain bad luck? I had a lot of time on my hands to weigh up answers to those questions.

I was born in Ashington in 1986, but my family moved to a nearby village called Lynemouth where I spent the first eight years of my life. We moved back to live in Ashington again, and that's where I spent the rest of my childhood, apart from a couple of years in Bedlington. Basically, I'm an Ashington lad.

Ashington is a former mining town in Northumberland, 15 miles up the road from Newcastle. It's probably best known as the home of legendary Newcastle United striker Jackie Milburn and the World Cup-winning Charlton brothers, Jack and Bobby. A lot of residents say they are sick of the place, and the media always highlights the negative aspects of my town, instead of the positive. Social media doesn't help. Everyone wants a good moan instead of getting involved and trying to improve the place. People tend to see only the bad side of my town, but it's my town, my home, and I am proud of it. I don't want to move away or live anywhere else.

Ashington has a real sense of community, and I've been lucky enough to experience that togetherness first-hand. Because of my imprisonment and the campaign to get me released, I saw how people from my home town came together to help spread the word about my plight and to support our campaign. I am incredibly grateful to them for that.

Most people were brilliant with me, and they still are. These days, I am stopped on the street by folks who ask me how I am. They wish me well, and I'll always have a chat. It's lovely. I don't always recognise people at first, but they'll have seen me on the telly or in the papers, so they know who I am. If they've known me a long time, I can tell which era of my life they come from by what they call me. When I was a little kid, I was Nicholas, then, when I was older, it was Nicky, and now Nick. Either that, or I get my nickname from my mates, which is Dunny. That's fine, I suppose, even though it is Australian slang for a toilet.

Nearly everyone in the town is positive, though a minority of people are stand-offish. There are always some folks who assume we must have been guilty of something. They pop up most often in the comments section under online news items involving the Chennai Six. They hide behind made-up usernames and post moronic theories about what we must have *really* done to have landed a prison sentence. They have no clue about our situation and have never seen or heard any evidence of wrongdoing, but that doesn't stop them from accusing us of being gun runners or mercenaries, all on the flimsy grounds that there is no smoke without fire. It's the "mercenary" tag that really annoys me. The difference between a mercenary and someone working in private security is vast. A mercenary is someone who is paid to fight in a foreign army. I was in the British Army, and the rest of the Chennai Six all served too. Between us, we had something like 70 years of combined service to our country.

None of us was a mercenary. We just used the skills we had learned to move into private security. In that industry, we had to undergo training and become accredited before we could take on contracted work. Our job was not to shoot or kill people. Our job was protection. Even when I was in the Paras, I wasn't a killer. Yes, when I went to a war zone, it could have been a case of kill-or-be-killed, but for the majority of my time the job was protection. In private security, we had the same role, but we didn't wear a uniform. That was the only difference.

None of this will stop deluded idiots from posting their ludicrous conspiracy theories online. One bloke accused of me being a drug dealer. He was convinced I had been selling Mexican steroids. I thought, "Aye mate, I got them from El Chapo."

That's one of the reasons I have put together this book. I want to explain what actually happened to us, and to set the record straight. As is often the case, the truth of what happened to us is crazier than fiction. You really couldn't make this up.

My childhood was pretty normal. I grew up with my family. My mam is called Margaret and my dad is James Dunn, but he prefers to be called Jim. They divorced in 1999, but they have always kept things as amicable as possible. Every week since my mam became ill, my dad has made her Sunday dinner. That says something about how much they still mean to each other. I'm close to both of them, and they suffered a great deal while I was imprisoned in India. As well as my sister, Lisa, I also have a brother called Paul, who is 10 years older than me.

I wish the kids of today could have a childhood like mine. We were always out doing something, not stuck indoors on phones or tablets. We would be playing football in all weathers, or down the woods exploring. I'd go off on long bike rides with my friends and, because we didn't have phones, there was no way of keeping tabs on us. We weren't expected to call home unless we were staying at a friend's house for our tea, or we were stopping over for the night.

That's all changed now, and people don't let their kids out of their sight any more because of the fear that something bad might happen. It's a sign of the times, but also a shame, because kids are missing out on some great adventures.

When I was growing up, both my parents worked, so I had to take care of myself. I learned to be self-reliant from an early age. We were still looked after, and my parents taught us strong values. I would be trusted to go out all day as long as I was home before dark. If I did something wrong, I knew I would get brayed, and I was taught to respect my elders. I see kids these days standing around outside McDonald's or the sports centre doing nothing, and I think to myself, what the hell are you playing at? It all seems so pointless.

I was no lover of school. I wasn't really academic and, as for my attendance – let's just say, some days I'd be there and other days not. School didn't really suit me. That's true for a lot of army lads. Maybe we are just too restless, or we can only focus and learn something if we think it's going to be of practical use.

I was a little, skinny lad, but I was never bullied. If there was ever any hassle, I always gave as good as I got, and I was no pushover. But I was not a fighter either. I'm still not really, unless you give me a weapon.

I always wanted to join the army, and I decided that, if that was the course I was going to take, I might as well try to join the best. I'd heard of the Marines, so I investigated some more and discovered they were connected to the navy not the army – and they had a height restriction. You had to be at least 5ft 6ins, and I was just under that. People think I'm taller because I'm bulky, but it's an illusion. I'm short for a soldier. The average is about 5ft 10ins.

I still wanted to join the best and the army didn't seem to care about my height. I couldn't go straight into the SAS, but I was still ambitious. At the Recruitment Centre in Ashington, I was told I could either join the Paras, sign up for the local regiment – the Fusiliers – or become an army chef. I said I wanted to go for the Paras. The recruiting sergeant said, "You do know they throw themselves out of aeroplanes? Are you scared of heights?"

I said, "No. I'm only scared of hitting the ground."

CHAPTER 4

P COMPANY

If I wanted to join the army, I would have to take an aptitude test called a Barb (British Army Recruitment Battery). That was designed to discover how intelligent candidates were, so the army could figure out where to send them. Since I'm as thick as a plank of wood, the best destination for me was definitely the Paras. For a start, I would have to be pretty daft to chuck myself out of an aeroplane, wouldn't I? The questions were straightforward, most were common sense, and I made it through OK.

I still had the option of trying for my local regiment, the Fusiliers, but the Paras immediately appealed to me. They were in a different league from the regular infantry, in my opinion. The Parachute Regiment was one of the elite units of the British Army and contained some of the best soldiers in the world. I wanted to see how tough I was, and if I could become part of this very demanding brotherhood.

It probably helped my decision that the Fusiliers had a very dodgy-looking cap decorated with a red and white plumed monstrosity called a Hackle. I could never imagine myself wearing that. Instead, I wanted to earn myself the coveted maroon beret.

Most people who joined the Parachute Regiment could barely tie their shoelaces. They were a bunch of renegades looking for somewhere to belong and hoping they had finally found a place they could call home. I was the same. But, by the time the regiment was done with us, we would have the skills and temperament needed to deal with just about any challenge. That was training I was glad of every day I was a prisoner in Chennai. The Parachute Regiment motto is *Utrinque Paratus*, which is Latin and means "Ready for Anything". It summed up the Para attitude to life and battle – and there were times in India when that resolve was put to the sternest test.

When I signed up, I learnt about the Paras' tough and demanding selection course that culminated in eight rigorous exercises over five days. This was the famous P Company. I was a short and skinny little whippersnapper. I figured the army would either destroy me completely or break me down then build me back up again. I would soon find out either way. I waited impatiently for my letter summoning me to join up. When it finally arrived, I went back to the career's office, this time with my family. My parents had to be there to give their approval because I was still only 17 when I swore the oath to my Queen and Country. It was an incredibly proud moment for me. I was standing there, staring at the officer. With my hand on the Bible, I recited the oath, dressed in my best suit. "Smart as a Guard and twice as hard," as we'd say in the Paras.

I was planning to join the Parachute Regiment as close as possible to my 18th birthday on 1 March 2004, but my paperwork was delayed. I ended up going a month later, during the first week in April. My family came to see me off at Newcastle train station. I'd never left home before. I was apprehensive, but also excited at the prospect of taking on this challenge and hopefully growing up a lot in the process. I thought, I'm 18 and it's time for me to leave my family and get on with my life, but, at the back of my mind, I was also worried in case the Paras took one look and decided they didn't want me. What if I failed the selection process? It would feel like I had let myself down, and my family too.

I didn't have to travel far to join the Paras. The selection process took place at the Infantry Training Centre at Catterick Garrison in North Yorkshire, so I got off the train at Darlington and caught a bus for the rest of the way. I rocked up to the main gates at the Helles barracks, presented myself to the Gurkha who was on guard, and told him I was joining up. I was directed to my new barracks and then had to endure the nerve-racking experience of watching everybody else arrive. These guys were all there for the same reason as me. I knew the Paras weren't going to take all of us, so they were my competition. There were some tough men too, including some big South African guys and massive Fijians. They were hard-looking blokes, and I was definitely one of the youngest and smallest. This was the beginning of a journey that would lead to P Company and those eight gruelling tests. Even though I was determined not to be intimidated, I was thinking, "What have I let myself in for?"

Eventually, I got to know some of the lads and did befriend one or two. We were supposed to work as a team, but everyone was mostly focussing on themselves and making sure they were the ones to qualify. I learned that the sergeant major was a man from my own home town of Ashington. This added to the pressure, but it made me more determined to show what I could do. I didn't want to let him down. At first, I thought he was very intimidating, but when I got to know him, I realised he was a regular guy.

We spent the first few weeks in barracks until we "passed off the square". That time was a test in itself, to see if we could hack being away from home. Every morning the NCOs (non-commissioned officers) made us switch off our phones and put them in a box. We wouldn't get them back until the end of the day. God help us if the phone was still on while it was in that box, because the NCOs would make us read out our messages in front of everyone. Depending on the contents, that could get embarrassing. Sometimes the phones went off, and they made us put the incoming call on speakerphone so everyone could hear. If that was your mother on the line, the sergeant or corporal might interrupt and take up the conversation. You can imagine how cringeworthy it might get if you're a young lad and your mother starts telling a hard-as-nails corporal, "I hope you are looking after my little boy." When that kind of thing happened, the sledging from the NCOs and the lads was merciless.

The No.2 haircut at the beginning of our training was another opportunity to tear us apart. Afterwards, there was a shout of "corridor", and we had to run and line up, all of us looking like a bunch of skinheads. The NCOs went down that line and everyone was picked up on something. No-one escaped. It was like a scene out of that brutal Vietnam war film, Full Metal Jacket.

"How old are you?"

"20, sergeant."

"No, you're not. You can't be! You look about 40! You must have had a fucking hard paper-round!"

That was a typical exchange. If you were short, tall, thin or broad, had a big nose or goofy teeth, they would point it out to you. But it was all just banter, and the NCOs were calling us out for a reason. They were testing to see if we could take a verbal beating. My attitude was "bring it on". I didn't care what they said. My height and build were the way they tried to get at me. "You're a skinny little wretch," I was told. "We are going to have fun with you."

I could take it though, and that was what the instructors wanted to see. They needed to know I was the kind of person who could respond to an enemy sending 10 rounds my way by firing 20 back. That didn't mean I would ever back-chat an NCO though. I'm not entirely stupid.

The instructors were putting us in a place where they had complete control over us – and for a good reason. They needed to instil in us the right attitude. Bayonet training was a horrible example. They were shouting at us the whole time that we were stabbing away, hammering home the need to be aggressive. They constantly reminded us that if we didn't kill the person on the other end of that bayonet, he would kill us.

Being made to crawl across a river bed through the icy cold water might not be a lot of fun, but in a battle, it might be the best option. We had to be ready. If there was machine gun or mortar fire coming at us, did we want to take our section over open ground with no cover? Or crawl through freezing water and sheep shit to save lives? There was no contest – but we had to be prepared. In the Paras, they trained us to go from A to B in the fastest, safest way possible, and to get the job done.

During those first six weeks of basic army training, I just had to keep my head down and get on with it. They made us wear a stupid cap that had inherited an obscene name because, when it's folded and viewed from above, the creases make it resemble a... well, I'm sure you can guess why it's called a C-Cap in mixed company. I couldn't wait to finish basic and get rid of that bloody cap. I had my sights set on the maroon beret the whole time. Once I'd mastered drill and other aspects of military discipline, I "passed off the square" and finally got my hands on a beret, but there was a twist: it had a green backing to show I was not a paratrooper yet. Not by a bloody long way.

That was when the selection course really got going, and it was tough. In particular, I found it hard to learn to tab, which was one of the key skills of a Para. Tab or "tactical advancement into battle" was a fast-paced march carrying kit and lasting for miles. Each recruit had to prove they could complete a 10-mile route, carrying a 35kg Bergen rucksack and a rifle, in under one hour 50 minutes. Royal Marines called their version "yomping", but what we did was "tabbing". I don't care what anyone says, we did it better and faster. That was why the Paras won the race to liberate Port Stanley in the Falkland Islands in 1982, not our softer rivals from the navy.

I had an extra burden because I kept suffering injuries to my knees and hips. Those who were injured could easily lose time, so the instructors were likely to put them back into a different platoon, which was frustrating. I was just beginning to understand exactly what was at stake, and I wanted it badly. So, when I picked up a serious injury, a possible stress fracture in my pelvis, I had to make a painful decision. I was put on crutches for a while, and it was gut-wrenching to hobble around while all the other blokes were giving it a go without me. I didn't want to give up and wait another 12 weeks to try all over again. I made up my mind. I went to the medical centre and threw down my crutches. I said, "I don't want these." I was limping back to barracks when I bumped into the platoon sergeant. He asked me where my crutches were. I said, "I don't need them any more. I want to be a Para." I half expected him to bollock me or tell me not to be so stupid, but I think he recognised and respected my determination. He didn't say anything, and he let me go.

I persevered and made sure everyone could see how determined I was to pass P Company. Soon, I found myself at the front of the line doing the 10-milers. When instructors asked me what I was doing up there, I'd always give them the same answer – "I want to be a Paratrooper!"

In depot training, there were some good guys and others I couldn't stand, but we knew we were all in this together. We had to work on two levels. We had to think as team players while, at the same time, pursuing our own individual goals: to get that maroon beret on our heads by any means possible. Some men did well on all the exercises but still failed because of their attitude. Others failed but kept coming back again and again until eventually they made it through. I was determined to pass first time with no mistakes.

The most important part of the selection process was the week-long event at the climax of the training. It consisted of eight tests designed to see if we had what it took to become a paratrooper.

The total score required to pass was 45 with 10 points maximum for each test, with marks awarded for qualities such as determination, aggression and leadership.

Each test was absolutely gruelling. We had two weeks to build up our fitness, and then we were pitched right into it. The rules were simple: if you didn't do well, you were gone. The army would not hesitate to kick out any candidate who didn't have the physical endurance and mental strength needed to join an elite unit.

P Company, otherwise known as P-Coy or, to give its full name, "Pegasus Company", after the winged-horse emblem closely associated with the Parachute Regiment, was about to test our strength, stamina and desire to breaking point.

The first test was the 10-miler, a march carrying a 35lb Bergen and a rifle. This had to be completed in under one hour 50 minutes. A few failed this one by not finishing in the required time but, in that case, it was still possible to pass the week if they showed the drive and determination the regiment was looking for. The march was fast-paced, but we were lucky. It was January, and the conditions were cool and dry. It was hard, but I wanted it a lot more than some of the others, and I made sure I passed.

The Trainasium was possibly the scariest part of P Company for most candidates. It was a big obstacle course built off the ground, reaching 18 metres (60ft) at its highest point. Being scared of heights was not the best qualification for a paratrooper, so this event was a straight pass or fail. If anyone messed this up, they were gone, with no second chance. Highlights of the Trainasium included the Illusion jump, so-called because it was a downwards jump that gave the illusion you were jumping further than you thought you were. A lot of people bottled it.

The Superman jump was another infamous test, and this was the cause of the most horrific incident I witnessed during my time in depot training. We were supposed to run and jump over a gap while punching out like we were Superman. Unfortunately, one of our number either didn't listen properly or he panicked and, instead of just punching out an arm, he pushed out his foot as well. It got caught in the netting and his ankle snapped on impact. We all heard the sickening crack. That was him finished. No-one could come back from an injury like that.

Once they had taken him away, our furious instructors halted the Trainasium, brought us all back inside, and lined us all along the corridor. They could tell some of the blokes were rattled after witnessing such an horrendous injury. One of the NCOs threw a boot all the way down the corridor for everyone to see. It was the one that had been cut from the injured man and it was still covered in the blood from his ruined ankle.

"That's what happens when you don't do your jobs properly!" hollered the NCO. "You end up like him!"

He wasn't exaggerating. Another guy fell off the Trainasium and damaged a vertebrate. It was not a game for the faint-hearted. The NCOs were right though, and I trusted them. I was apprehensive after what I had seen, but when the instructors said jump, I knew

I would have to jump, or I'd never become a Para. Simple as. If I jumped with commitment, I'd make it. If I'd jumped like a fanny, I would injure myself. It was called a confidence test for a reason, and I had confidence in myself and the instructors, so I made it through. In fact, I thought the Trainasium was a piece of piss. It was basically a big kids' playground. If you could handle standing on some bars, 18 metres up, while being told to touch your toes and shout out your name and number, then you could get through, no probs. I've never had an issue with heights.

The log race was a team event where eight men had to carry a 60kg telegraph pole for 1.9 miles. The instructors were looking for us to show determination and leadership, and I reckon I demonstrated both. The bloke next to me was seriously flagging and wanted to stop, but I was there to urge him on and keep him going. I was determined my team would win that race and we did, comfortably. In fact, we blew the other team out of the water. I was knackered afterwards, but we had all knuckled down and listened to the staff. We had stayed together as a team, and we had done it.

Next up was the two-mile march. Once again, we were wearing helmets and carrying a 35lb Bergen and a rifle. We were tracking up and down hills but, this time, each candidate was in their own race. It was an individual not a group pursuit, and it was gruelling because we only had 18 minutes. My plan was to set off as part of the group and then keep pace with the PTI (physical training instructor). This challenge was all about who wanted it most. Everyone was looking out for themselves. As for keeping up with the PTI, there was no chance. I couldn't keep up with the pack either and, before the end, I was blowing out of my arse. But I finished within the time limit though. Just.

The steeplechase was a two-mile, cross-country run, immediately followed by an assault course. There was no kit to carry, but we wore heavy army boots. It was wet, muddy, cold and downright horrible, especially when we were breaking ice on the water obstacles. I had to find another level, mentally and physically, to see it through. It was an individual, timed event, and I had to give maximum effort to pass. Again, I was successful.

Most people have heard about milling. Prospective Paras had to show "controlled physical aggression" during an event that looked like a boxing match but couldn't be further from one. That was because there were no marks for ducking or avoiding the other guy's punches. Instead, combatants would lose marks for backing off. Our only protection was a head guard, a gum shield and boxing gloves. We were meant to be paired with someone who was roughly our own height and build, but the instructors had a bit of problem with me because everyone else was so much bigger. I was left standing on my own in the corridor with no opponent. The NCOs sized me up, and one of them said, "I know, I'll go and fetch my daughter. She's only little."

In the end they paired me with a mate, Foggy. He'd already fought once, but they made him take on me too because he was the only one remotely close to my build. But he was still bigger and, unfortunately for me, a very good boxer. He hit hard.

Milling was designed to see what we were made of when we were under attack, which was why the instructors demanded we didn't flinch, duck, or run away. They expected us to take the blows and land our own. If someone started shooting at us in battle, Paras were expected to respond aggressively. It was another event to drill home the message: if someone sent 10 rounds our way, we would send 20 right back. Milling was like that, but with fists instead of bullets. We took this beating in front of everyone. There was no hiding place. We were told to go at it for 60 seconds, and I was just about ready for that when the corporal suddenly said, "You wear contact lenses don't you Dunn? I suggest you take them out to make it more interesting."

I said, "But corporal, if I take them out, I won't be able to see anything."

He replied, "And that's what will make it more interesting."

So, there I was, half blind and swinging punches at a tough bloke I could barely see. Being a decent boxer, Foggy landed more punches than me. In fact, I got a pasting, and he made a mess of my nose in the process, but I landed a few on him too. Crucially, I didn't back off or duck from anything he sent my way – and that wasn't just because I couldn't see his punches coming!

Once the milling was over, we went straight into the weekend break. Foggy was an Ashington lad too and, with superb timing, we had already planned to head home for a night out on the beer in our home town. Luckily, neither of us had too many cuts and bruises on our faces, so the pubs still let us in.

When we were back after the weekend break, we were immediately sent off on a 20-mile endurance march. We had four hours 10 minutes to complete this and, once again, we were carrying that 35lb Bergen and a rifle. I tabbed the whole way and, as I was getting good at the technique by now, I knew the challenge was well within my capabilities. In fact, it became almost boring. It felt like a 20-mile slow march for most of the time and that was for a reason. The idea was to demonstrate endurance, and I had no problem meeting that challenge.

I wish I could say the final event was just as straightforward. The stretcher race was an absolute bastard. Teams of 16 had to lug a 175kg stretcher for five miles wearing webbing and carrying a weapon. Because of my height, I had to pull the stretcher right onto my shoulder but, no matter what I did, it kept sliding off. All of us were struggling to keep up, and it was even harder for me because I was the smallest. Other people were falling away, but I was determined to stay on as long as possible because I knew how important this final test was going to be. There were always four on the stretcher at any one time. We were supposed to rotate, but I made sure I was always among the four the whole time because I was keen to make a positive impression. It got so bad I was in tears but, somehow, I managed to keep going. That was what was expected of us – they didn't want quitters in the Paras. When I crossed that line, I had given everything. I was mentally and physically exhausted.

When the week-long event was finally over, the instructors assembled all of the guys who were still standing. We were about to find out if we had passed or failed. It was a nerve-racking moment, but there wasn't much formality about the cut. They just called out our numbers, we stood to attention, and they said either "pass" or "fail". My number was 10. When I heard the instructors call it out, I rose to my feet, came to attention, and heard the word I wanted to hear. "Pass."

The relief flooded through me. I'd done it! I hadn't let down myself, or my family. I had made it through one of the toughest military selection processes in the world on my first attempt, and I hadn't failed a single event, not one. I was finally a Para. I might not have been a big bloke, but when I got through P Company, believe me, I was 10ft tall.

Only one or two lads failed at the very end, but lots had fallen by the wayside long before then. They either couldn't hack it physically or mentally, or they couldn't come back from injury. What I went through during the selection process was character-building, and it was necessary to toughen me up. I have no doubt that the training and the resilience I learnt helped to save my life in India.

Once I had passed P Company, I was officially classed as a paratrooper. I could finally remove that bloody green backing from my maroon beret and wear it with pride. There were only live exercises to come before we were allowed to pass out for the final time in front of our family at Catterick. On that day, I was marching on the outside of the three ranks, the closest to the stadium, so my family could see me when we paraded off the square to Ride of the Valkyries, our signature tune.

They were all really proud of me. My dad even filmed the event on one of those old-school video recorders. That was a very proud moment for me too. The boy had become a man.

CHAPTER 5

LIFE AS A PENGUIN

Prison anywhere in the world is the same. It comes down to an endless routine, every day seeming just like the last. Jails might thrive on the order that provides, but prisoners will do anything to vary their days and break the boredom.

The lows I experienced while I was banged up in Chennai came in many forms, but the highs usually involved contact from home. When I received a message or letter, I knew I hadn't been forgotten by family and friends. A letter was a big deal, and a parcel a major event. I can't tell you how good it felt to receive something from the outside, especially when it came all the way from the UK. The contents of a parcel were always welcome. We couldn't exactly pop out to the shops when we were banged up and, even if we could, there was a lot of stuff that just wasn't available in Chennai. But that wasn't the point – it was more about the effect on morale, knowing that someone had cared enough to go to the trouble of buying the items, putting together a parcel, and arranging to have it sent to India. It meant such a lot when I was stuck thousands of miles away in a foreign jail, worrying that everyone might eventually forget about me. It was so important for my peace of mind. When a parcel arrived, it was always a good day.

That's why I will always think highly of my old Para mate, Gary Hull. He never forgot about me, and sent a food parcel every month. He was an amazing support to us all, and he never let up trying to raise awareness of our predicament wherever he went. Gary had left the Paras and went on to own a scaffolding business. Whenever he took on a new job, he would place posters on the scaffolding alerting everybody to the plight of the Chennai Six. One day, he was erecting some scaffolding outside a veterinary practice. The vet came out and complained that the posters were obscuring his premises. Gary said that the scaffolding was doing that anyway, so it made no difference. He then calmly explained who we were and the huge miscarriage of justice we had endured. The miserable bloke listened, but he made it clear he didn't care. He demanded that the posters be taken down. As soon as Gary heard that, he took everything down – posters, scaffolding, the lot – and he walked off the job, leaving the bloke in the lurch. He would have to find someone else to do the work.

It didn't matter how busy Gary was, he always made the time to buy a big brown envelope from the Post Office and then stuff in as many things as he could, before posting the package off to me. Somehow, he'd manage to squeeze 15, or even 20, items into that A3-sized envelope. The postage alone must have cost him £20, and the envelopes took at least a week to reach me, but he kept them coming all the time I was out there. I will never forget his kindness.

An Indian inmate we called "Postie" would come by with his little notebook and say, "You have parcel," or "You have letter". We'd head straight down to the jailer's office to collect whatever had arrived. Postie would write down the contents of the parcel, and the jailer would check for contraband or any item that could be used as a weapon. When that was done, the jailer would say "OK", and I could finally take possession of my parcel.

It wasn't easy to mail food from the UK all the way to India. Our friends and family couldn't send anything that might melt in the heat, like chocolate, or fresh fruit that would perish before it arrived. Anything that might make our usual food taste better, like dry seasoning or herbs, was a bonus. And it was always a treat to get something sweet that could survive the journey, like a bag of Haribo. My favourite food presents of all were sachets of John West tuna. I used to thoroughly enjoy them.

The best item Gary sent to me wasn't food. One day, I opened a letter and inside was an invitation to his wedding. He will never know the positive effect that had on me. It gave me a new sense of determination to get out of there. I remember saying to myself that I had to be free by next year or I'd miss my mate's big day. That invitation gave me hope and something to look forward to, which was so important at a time when we were usually just trying to get through the day. It was a long-term goal that spurred me on and made me even more determined to survive this hell.

I'd known Gary ever since I was 19, and we were deployed to Northern Ireland together in 2005. Every time I received a parcel from him, it reminded me of our earliest days in the regiment together, shortly after I passed recruitment. At that point, I was officially a paratrooper, but I didn't yet have the all-important wings because I hadn't done my jumps. Once I had passed out, I was allowed some leave, and I went home for a while. I was ordered to keep in contact with the Guard Room, so I'd know straight away when I was going to RAF Brize Norton to tackle my jumps and finally get my wings. I was told there would be a bus to get me down to Oxfordshire, and it was very important I didn't miss it. I kept calling and waiting for the nod. For some reason, the regiment made a mistake and gave me the wrong date and time, so the bloody bus left without me. I figured I would have to make my own way to Oxfordshire, but before I had a chance to worry about new transport arrangements, there was a change of plan. The sergeant major told me to get to Dover instead. He ordered me to join up with 1 Para – even though I was wing-less.

I turned up late one evening at the Guard Room in Dover with all my gear. I was shitting myself because I had a feeling nobody knew I was coming. It turned out I was right. The first thing the Guard Commander asked me was, "Who the fuck are you?"

I explained to this corporal that I was a new recruit to 1 Para, but that didn't help much. My unexpected arrival was an unwelcome distraction. The whole battalion was in the final stages of preparing to deploy to Northern Ireland, and there was still a lot of admin and logistics to sort out before they went. The Paras had far more pressing things on their mind than me. This was going to be the last time the Parachute Regiment would be deployed in Northern Ireland, and everything had to be right.

At least they managed to find me a spare bunk. A sergeant put me inside a tiny room on my own and told me when and where to report the next day. In the morning, I could see the base in daylight.

There was hardly anyone about because nearly everyone was away on deployment training. I was now officially in B Company, but more or less on my own. I used the time to carry out weapons testing and zero in my SA80 assault rifle while I waited for the rest of the lads to return.

I ended up doing my Northern Ireland induction training later, on a Royal Green Jackets base, and it was a piece of piss compared to P Company. I was put together with a few other guys, although I was the only one with no wings. They all cottoned on I was new, but most of them were OK about it and didn't treat me any differently. I did a couple of months in Northern Ireland with no wings, and it didn't seem to bother most people – although one of the corporals was a proper little arsehole about it. He was the only one who gave me any grief but, of course, I couldn't escape the usual Para piss-taking and banter. I knew it was technically possible to join a battalion before I had done the jumps that fully qualified me as a paratrooper, but there would be consequences, and it would be a cause for comment. For a start, I was called "Penguin" because I didn't have wings and I wasn't really "airborne". The penguin noises would come at me every time I walked by the lads. After the sledging I had taken during Para training, this wasn't anything new, and I didn't give a shit. I could hack it – but I couldn't help wishing I'd been given the chance to jump before I joined 1 Para, so I felt less like an imposter.

The Northern Ireland I experienced on my first deployment in 2005 was very different from the one most people imagine when they think of the "Troubles" – that mild word for 30 years of sectarian hatred and violence. The British Army lost more than

600 men in the conflict with the IRA but, by the time we were patrolling out there, the peace process had been under way for a number of years, and a ceasefire was in place. I didn't have to walk the streets of Belfast either, as we were deployed 40 miles away at South Armagh, which was huge and very rural. There were other differences too. We wore berets instead of helmets. We had our weapons, but we didn't look like we were going out to stir up a fight. We were still briefed about local figures in PIRA (Provisional Irish Republican Army), so we knew who the key players were, but we never had to engage with anyone while on a patrol.

On a few occasions, we found a cache of weapons, but they were always old. The people responsible for them had probably been arrested long before, and the weapons had been abandoned where they had been hidden. Usually they were just buried in a field. We would get some intelligence about a location and go down to retrieve them. Quite often, we got the intel from "Clouts", Irish Catholic, IRA supporters who had been turned by the Brits for whatever reason. Sometimes they had broken the law but were left alone if they gave us a bit of information.

It was a different time and a different place compared to the height of the Troubles, but we still had to be on our guard. Some of the civilians were OK, although kids would occasionally throw stones at us and call us names. They'd shout racist stuff at the Fijians, and I would get called a dwarf, which didn't bother me at all. I did have one funny incident in Northern Ireland, but it would have been no laughing matter if the same thing had happened when the shit hit the fan for real in Afghanistan or Iraq.

Somehow, and I still don't know how, I broke the safety catch on my SA80, which meant I would have been zero use in a gunfight. I was effectively weapon-less. The NCOs were stunned, because no one could imagine how I had managed to do it. I was called "a fucking idiot" and asked, "How has that happened?" I couldn't tell them, because I didn't know. Even now, it chills me to think what could have happened if my weapon had failed me when I needed it most.

All in all, Northern Ireland was OK. It was my first tour. I didn't have too much time to get into battalion life, and it all went by in a bit of a blur – but there was one major milestone. During my time there, I was finally given the order to get my wings.

Weeks after the time I was supposed to go to Brize Norton to chuck myself out of an aeroplane, I finally arrived at the base to take the Basic Parachute Course. It was a strange reversal of the usual routine as I'd already been deployed on a tour as a Para. As a result, I had to make sure I didn't make a mess of this or all my experiences would have been for nothing. I couldn't be a paratrooper if I failed to complete my jumps, so this wasn't the time to suddenly develop a fear of heights.

With my usual crap luck, I ended up staying on the base longer than I should have. The weather wasn't great, and it was too windy for jumping. Brize Norton was a big RAF camp, and we were far from the only ones on the base. Planes were going off to Iraq and Afghanistan all the time, and I realised that one day, before too long, that was probably going to be me.

When the weather finally lifted, we set off for our first jump, taking off in a C-130 Hercules. As I shuffled on board, I didn't really think about the jump itself, I was just concentrating on what "stick" – or group – I was in, and whether I was sitting port or starboard. There was no time to reflect on what came next. Everyone climbed on board and I happened to be the last one on. It took some time before I realised this meant I would be the first one off too.

It would have been far better if someone had gone ahead of me so I could get an idea of what to expect. Instead, I was about to go out of the door for my very first jump having no real idea what would happen apart from what they had taught us in training. The instructors told us about the routines – instilling techniques for exiting the plane, disentangling lines if we had to, and landing without breaking anything. That was great in theory, but jumping from an aircraft 1,000ft feet up was not quite the same. When it finally dawned on me that I was going to be first, I thought "oh fuck" – but there wasn't a great deal of time to dwell on it or get too nervous, which was probably just as well.

There was a shout of "action stations", and we all stood. We hooked on the static line, made sure it was secure, and then everyone counted down from the back until it was my turn. Then it was "One OK, stick OK!" until the PJI (parachute jumping instructor) was finally happy.

I stood at the open door of the Hercules, staring down at the ground 1,000ft below. The instructor had his hand on my back, and I waited. When the green light came on, he gave me the signal, and I launched myself from the aircraft into nothing.

I was out of the plane and falling. The slipstream hit me, and I had no control. Then, thankfully, the static line did its job, and my chute suddenly opened. My training kicked in, and I looked up to check the canopy was open and there were no twists in the lines. The chute looked fine. British parachutes were some of the best in the world, and I had confidence in mine. I'm also a pretty fatalistic person, so I figured what would be would be and, if the chute didn't open, then there wasn't much I could do about it. There was no point worrying.

Once I knew that my parachute had opened successfully, I looked down and enjoyed the jump. I could see fields far below and traffic going by underneath me. I felt very alive to be out there so high up, slowly falling towards the ground in such a controlled way. I can honestly say I was not afraid. I landed OK, and we went out again in the afternoon. I had to complete a minimum of five jumps while I was at Brize Norton in order to qualify as a military parachutist and, once they were over, I was finally given my wings. I was 19 years old and I had been in the army for 14 months. Finally, I could properly call myself a Para.

The Parachute Regiment is famous for these jumps, but there's a strange truth to the tradition – we don't do them on operations any more. They are too dangerous for a number of reasons. Men can be injured during the jump, or they could be scattered by wind and end up separated, or they could hit the ground miles from the landing zone. Usually there is no actual need to be dropped in for a mission. In fact, the last time a battalion of the Paras jumped together in a hostile environment was during the Suez Crisis way back in the 1950s. These days, Paras are far more likely to be deployed in land vehicles, from helicopters, or on foot.

In a way, the jumps are a test of courage, to see if you have the balls to do them, as well as an important link to the Parachute Regiment's history and heritage. I've jumped at 600ft in the dark with full kit and landed with a twisted chute with no time to make any corrections. I just had to accept the hard landing that would follow. The first time I had twists, I managed to sort out the tangle, but on the second occasion I was too low and ran out of time. The ground rushed up to meet me, and the hard landing knocked the wind right out of me. Luckily, I didn't break anything. I did two jumps at night, one from 1,000ft, one from 600ft, a couple without kit, and one with a Bergen full of blocks to add weight. I've completed 13 jumps in my career, and I enjoyed them all, but I never had to make a jump as part of an op, even when we were supporting the SAS.

CHAPTER 6

SPECIAL OPS TRAINING & AFGHANISTAN

From Ireland, we went back to Dover before packing up and moving to MoD St Athan in Glamorgan, South Wales, in February 2006. The battalion was based there to be close to Special Forces who trained nearby. We were given six months counter-terrorism training as part of Special Forces Support Group (SFSG), taking instruction on additional weapons and specialist assault skills.

Many people still remember the Iranian Embassy siege in 1980, and younger people will have at least seen the footage. The world watched on as the Special Air Service (SAS) stormed the embassy and saved the hostages. It was a prime example of the effectiveness of expertise, sharpened by rigorous training. At St Athan, instructors taught us how to enter a building the SAS way. We had to go in fast, wearing respirators, with our weapons ready to fire. We aimed at pop-up targets. This was made more challenging because some of the targets were "friends" – civilian hostages – that we were meant to be saving. Others were enemies – armed terrorists who would kill us, and the hostages, if we hesitated. We only had a split second to make a decision about who was who before firing at the right targets. We used paint rounds in training, but it was realistic enough for an exercise.

We were also taught how to join a fast-moving vessel in the water. We did this by fast-roping down from a helicopter, in full kit complete with respirator, straight onto the ship. We had to be very fast too. The guy before me took too long and ended up accidentally breaking my fall. I never did thank him! We'd leave afterwards on a RIB (rigid inflatable boat), a small, fast-moving vessel that pulled up alongside. We had to know how to fight in all conditions if we were going to fill our role supporting the SAS, who could be deployed anywhere in the world at short notice. We were rotated every six months, and we mirrored the squadron or troop of the SAS or SBS – Special Boat Service – we were linked to. One company was always on ops for six months, one on standby and one on pre-deployment training. We had to train and train well, giving it everything we had. Like the old army saying goes, "Train hard, fight easy." In our case, we trained for the worst so if the worst actually happened, and we had to deal with it for real, we had a much better chance of staying alive. When we trained, we didn't hold back. We went at it long and hard. To be the best we had to train like the best.

On training exercises, we'd often work with members of the SAS. Most of them were OK, but one or two of them could get lippy. For a time, some of them really hated us because we had become better at what we were doing than they were. If that sounds big-headed, it's not. We were the best infantry unit in the army. The SAS was a small band of men and the majority of them were ex-Paras. When we were given training, we would pick it up quickly, we'd be good at it, and we would only get better. We took it seriously, and we were driven to show the SAS guys we were competent, and they could rely on us. They were the best, so we had to be the best too.

In the end though, there was always a mutual respect between the Paras and the SAS. In fact, quite a few of our guys would go on to do Special Forces Selection. The army wanted 1 Para to be like the Special Forces we supported, although this caused some tension. Once we actually started looking or acting like them, we would be told to back off. "If you want to be that kind of soldier then go off and do the course," we were told.

On other operations, instructors went the other way and made us wear regimental tops and keep our hair short to show up the difference. The SAS guys thought that this was daft because we stood out. They asked, "Why are you lot in 1 Para in skinheads and reg tops when you are meant to blend in with Special Forces?" They reckoned we looked like we were straight out of P Company. It was frustrating and made little sense.

Previous SAS operations had convinced army top brass to create a specific support unit, which was the SFSG. But they didn't seem to want us to be fully immersed in the role. Instead, we played the part, but never really looked the part.

* * *

Chennai was one of the hottest places in India and the world. I never liked the heat, but at least I had experienced those conditions before, when I was in the Paras. There were many times in jail when I told myself it was just as well I'd been a member of 1

Para. Army life had given me the reserves of physical and mental resilience that I needed to survive. I was used to roughing it in ways civilians didn't usually encounter. I don't think it's an exaggeration to say that being a Para saved my life in Chennai.

At the time, people asked me if I was scared about going out to Afghanistan, but, in truth, I was excited about the prospect. No-one trained to be a soldier without wanting to go to a war zone. There was no point in having an army if we didn't go where the action was. Yes, of course, there were dangers, but facing down those dangers was our job. It was who we were and what we had trained to become.

I arrived in Afghanistan in July 2007 when the heat was hitting 40C. On a bad day, it would go even higher. Chennai's record temperature came in 2003, long before I was stuck there, when the thermometer hit 45C.

Our journey to Afghanistan started when we flew into Turkey. We refuelled and headed on to Kandahar in the south of the country, not far from the Pakistani border. The final stage involved flying to Camp Bastion in a Hercules – although this time I wouldn't be chucking myself out. When we reached the camp, it wasn't long before our long-standing resentment of the Royal Marines flared up again, and the friction all started over something pretty basic: hot water. Those dozy bastards kept running down the supply because they were forever taking showers. We had to tell them, "You're not on board a ship any more. You're on the ground now, and you have to make do with a packet of wet wipes and one shower a day, if you're lucky."

Most of the time, we made sure we didn't clash too much, but the tension between us was always simmering somewhere in the background. All of that went out of the window when we worked together in a war zone, but it never altered my opinion of them. As a fighting force they were good, but not as effective as us. In the Paras, we reckoned we were more direct. We'd be kicking in the door, smashing up an enemy and moving on while the Marines were still weighing up the options. We used to say Marines were thinkers – but we didn't mean that as a compliment. We reckoned they were ditherers, and that was why we jokingly called them "Maureens". Paras thought of ourselves as doers. We didn't waste time. We got on with the job we have been given, and we got it done.

It also seemed like the Marines weren't held to the same level of account as we were. While I was in Afghanistan, a Royal Marine lost his night vision goggles (NVG). If I had lost an important piece of equipment like that, there would have been serious consequences, but he got nothing, not even a basic bollocking. That piece of kit could have ended up in the hands of the Taliban – and equipping one of their snipers with NVG could have proved fatal for our guys. But the Marine got away with his carelessness and, as far as I know, he wasn't even punished.

Like I said, I didn't mind going to war, and I certainly wasn't scared to be sent out there but, by the time we were deployed, the Afghanistan situation was not really a conventional war at all. That was half the trouble. It was more like another Northern Ireland, only much worse. It was a disaster, in fact.

When I was out on an op as a soldier, I wasn't paid to think. I just did the job I'd been given without question. But I couldn't help noticing what was going on around me and, later, after I returned home, I wondered whether it had all been worth it or not. People died out there, and I was lucky because I wasn't one of them. It was a desolate, horrible country. Afghans lived their lives in a primitive way by western standards. In most places, they didn't even have schools for girls. We were out there to help them rebuild after years of conflict, but that proved difficult. Our primary job was to defeat the Taliban, but we also engaged in so-called hearts-and-minds campaigns to win the Afghan people over to our way of thinking. I would be sent to meetings with the locals where I would act as a guard while my officer talked to people about what could be done to improve their lives. I came to the conclusion these people didn't really want our help. It seemed to me that most of the population didn't want us there at all and our presence probably wouldn't make much difference in the long run. I started to wonder – what the fuck was I doing there?

Unfortunately, 'hearts-and-minds' was never going to be enough to win a war in Afghanistan. The Taliban operated across a huge country that was mountainous and complex, and their soldiers had a solid knowledge of the local terrain. They always seemed to know in advance when air support from Apache helicopters or fast jets was coming in, and then they'd just disappear into tunnels in the mountains and hide out. We couldn't find all of their tunnels no matter how many bombs we dropped. Putting boots on the ground was the only way to clear out enemy fighters, but that wasn't easy because the place had been mined to hell by the Russians during their invasion way back in the 1980s. The heat played a big part too, as fighting had to stop during the hottest part of the day.

During Ramadan, when our Muslims allies in the Afghan National Army couldn't eat during the day for religious reasons, their soldiers were lethargic and would only come to life again in the evening. It was part of my role to instruct and train these guys. I did my job because I was ordered to but, deep down, I felt no interest in training these people. They never fully gained my trust. I believed we were showing potentially hostile people how to be better at war and, sooner or later, there would be a price to pay if, for example, some of them went rogue and used their new skills against us. I was never surprised when supposedly friendly forces turned against British or American soldiers in tragic, fatal incidents. They occurred so often there was actually a term for it. When a member of the Afghan National Army shot a coalition soldier it was known as a "green-on-blue". Since my time in Afghanistan, three Grenadier Guards, two Military Police officers, three Gurkhas and a Royal Marine have been killed by so-called allies, either from the Afghan National Army or the police force, both of which have been compromised and infiltrated by the Taliban or their supporters.

It wasn't all bad though. I was working with good guys, and it was my job. It helped that we were not like the rest of the British Army. We were light years ahead, in fact. The equipment we were given was shit to begin with but, over time, the quality started to improve. And we had different and more dangerous roles to play, which made our time out there more interesting.

Sometimes we'd be on the ground for three weeks at a time. It was hard work and brought its own challenges, some of them surprising. I remember one day I had taken off my boot and I was airing my feet when suddenly a camel spider ran up and tried to bite me. These creatures were usually around six inches long, and this one seemed especially massive. Camel spiders were quick too, capable of running at up to 10mph. This big, ugly fucker was coming right at me! I got a shock but thankfully I didn't freeze. Instead, I jumped up, still wearing just the one boot, and I stamped on the bugger. Goodbye camel spider.

We were fighting an invisible enemy in Afghanistan. Their soldiers didn't want to engage with us at close quarters. Instead, they used to shoot and scoot. Often, by the time we responded and returned fire, they were gone. They knew the terrain well and would melt into the background. Sometimes I could see the Taliban snipers from a distance, but I couldn't tell what they were shooting at, even though I was staring right at them through binoculars. One day, another patrol clocked one of their snipers and decided to take him out with an FGM-148 Javelin, a man-mounted anti-tank missile. Our snipers were telling the Javelin guy where to fire. Now, a missile from a Javelin cost about £70,000, so if you fired that thing and missed, it wasn't going to go down well. The bloke was told to make sure he hit the target. No pressure! He fired and missed. So he tried again. He launched another Javelin and missed for a second time! He got absolutely ripped apart. Unsurprisingly, he was told he had been removed from Javelin duties.

During another patrol, I received a reminder of just how high the stakes were in Afghanistan. I heard on our radio that an officer had been shot. He was out of cover, surveying the ground ahead of him, and a sniper got him. Luckily, his guys had a good medic with them that day and they saved his life. He survived when others wouldn't be so fortunate. Between 2001 and 2015, 456 British personnel were killed in Afghanistan. It does make me wonder if that sacrifice was worth it.

If Afghanistan was bad for Britain, it was even worse for the Americans. It was essentially the Vietnam War all over again for them. It was as if they hadn't learned anything from the embarrassment of that defeat decades earlier, or from the experiences of the Soviet Union, which invaded Afghanistan back in the 1980s. The Soviets were stuck there for 10 long years and it was a bloody disaster. Now the Americans are trying to leave the place after more than 18 years, and they are struggling. I wasn't traumatised by my experiences, but I do think that fighting a war in Afghanistan is a pointless and unwinnable exercise. The place is too big, too wide open, and there is so much corruption everywhere, making Afghanistan virtually ungovernable. Every time we think we have secured a victory over the enemy, the Taliban fighters melt back across the Pakistani border. Maybe President Donald Trump should stop trying to build a wall to prevent immigrants entering the United States. Instead, he should persuade Pakistan to get building to stop the Taliban slipping in and out of Afghanistan. That's a border that could really use a wall.

CHAPTER 7

BLOWN UP!

In Chennai, it was the same haunting sound every night, and always at the same time. We would hear that eerie clattering of the keys in the door and the rattling of chains afterwards as the guard walked away. We knew we'd been locked in for another night. Every time it happened, I would wonder if that night was bringing me one step closer to going home, or whether I would be stuck here until everyone but my closest family had forgotten all about me. I told myself I had to believe I would be released eventually – but when would that be? And how much more of this hell would I be forced to endure?

After 6pm every night, we were all locked in together and there wasn't much to do for the rest of the evening except read a book or talk. I was locked up with Paul, Billy, John and Ray. Paul and Billy had been in 1 Para before I was there, John was in 3 Para, and Nick and Ray had both been in the 1st Battalion Yorkshire Regiment, where Ray had been a master sniper. This was the time when all the old funny anecdotes would come out, and we'd tell each other our "war stories" for entertainment. It was one of the few ways we had of passing the time. There I was, locked up in a jail in India, without the ability to get on with my life and, because of that, all the old times in Iraq and Afghanistan would come back to me. They would seem very real too, because I was sharing them with guys who had all experienced similar things. I did have a slight advantage in the story stakes though – I was the only guy in our cell who had ever been blown up.

The Parachute Regiment was always deployed at the sharp end and my time overseas was no exception. I served for six years and, for the majority of the time, I was either in Iraq or Afghanistan, with a stint in Northern Ireland too. I knew that, when I was deployed to a war zone, I would face the potential of serious harm, but I put that prospect out of my head and got on with my job. Even so, the thought that death might be just around the corner was always in the back of my mind – and, in Afghanistan, I came close. Very close.

Don't ask me to tell you exactly when I was blown up. I can't recall the date and, if you think that's strange, I have to say I don't really consider it to be the most important part of the story. Not dying was the only bit we cared about at the time. The Land Rover transporting us was destroyed by a mine when it was blown up – with us still in it.

There were times I spent in Chennai jail when I would look back on that moment and wonder if I had already used up all my luck. Perhaps being in prison, for a crime I did not commit, was fate's way of squaring the account somehow. On other occasions, that lucky escape made me more determined to make sure my life – which so easily could have been cut short that day – would be lived to the full, and not be wasted. I couldn't accept just rotting away in a cell in India. Not after all I'd been through. I had to get out of there, no matter what.

The day we were blown up began like any other. We met at the Final Rendezvous Point in Musa Qala, Helmand Province, before heading out as a group. B Company had been ordered to investigate reports of enemy combatants posing as locals in a nearby town. Our job was to root them out. We were sent to track down two guys, a father and son, who were nowhere to be seen by the time we arrived. Having failed to locate them, we returned to base, taking the same route back. There were three of us in a Land Rover WMIK. That stood for Weapons Mounted Installation Kit, but everyone just called it a WIMIK. Though we were on alert, as always, there was absolutely nothing to indicate we were about to be taken out in spectacular fashion.

All of a sudden, the relative calm was shattered by an almighty boom. We'd driven over a mine. The force of the blast rocked the vehicle. I was top gunner at the time, handling a General Purpose Machine Gun, a GIMPY. One moment I was there with the gun, and the next thing I knew, I was flat out in the back of the Land Rover wondering what the hell had just happened, dust flying all around.

In the immediate aftermath, there was no time to react. The incident was all over in a second. It reminded me of the movies: life really did feel like it was going in slow motion.

Once I realised I was still alive, I acted on instinct. The first thing I did was to reach down and check myself to make sure the "crown jewels" were still there. They were. Both of them. I was still a man. Huge relief all round. It was then I understood that I wasn't just alive, but I had been entirely uninjured by the blast. The other two guys in the jeep with me were unscathed too. How the hell had we been blown up, our jeep destroyed right out from under us, and yet none of us had been killed or badly injured? The odds against that were enormous. There had to be someone looking over us that day.

Instinct told us to get clear of the vehicle quickly, but the guys following behind knew that was a very bad idea. The area around us had to be checked thoroughly for more mines. I was about to scramble out the back when someone shouted, "Don't move!" I stayed where I was, even though I really wanted to be out of that crippled jeep sharpish.

Eventually, the area was cleared, and I jumped down. My legs were still shaking. We walked round to the front to see the damage to our Land Rover. By some bloody miracle, the force of the blast had gone straight up into the engine block, leaving a gaping hole where our engine used to be. We could look right down through the rip and see the ground beneath. A blast of that force would have done us serious damage if it had breached any other part of the vehicle. Christ, we were lucky. Later, we discovered we had driven over a pressure pad, which had triggered an anti-personnel mine designed to kill or maim a soldier, but not necessarily destroy a vehicle – though it still managed to do a pretty good job!

Then our professionalism took over. We couldn't just dump the Land Rover for the Taliban to scavenge. We kept calm and did not panic. The memory of that Marine who lost his NVGs stayed with me, and we made sure we didn't leave any equipment that could be turned against us one day. We stripped out everything until the vehicle was just a shell, then we blew up what was left.

There was one more twist. The blokes who checked the road for us found a far more powerful anti-tank mine very close by. If we had driven slightly further over to one side on that same stretch of track, we would have triggered a much bigger blast – one that would have ensured none of us survived.

We looked at each other then, each knowing how close we had just come to death. Our reaction? We had a good laugh and carried on. That's how we dealt with those experiences. It might seem strange to anyone who hasn't been through something like that, but it was the only way we could be. That was the reality of being in a war zone, and I can honestly say it didn't affect my outlook. I didn't let it. I couldn't. I just had to get on with my job.

CHAPTER 8

GETTING SHELLED

By July 2007, my deployment in Afghanistan was finally over. On the journey home we stopped off in Muscat, a city of over a million people and the port capital of Oman. We had a 14-hour layover between flights and, predictably, my first impulse was to go out and get pissed. I wasn't the only one. All of us had survived a dangerous tour of duty in hostile territory and we hadn't tasted an alcoholic drink in months.

There was a mixed bunch of us out on the lash during the layover, including Paras and Marines, which was always a recipe for carnage. Add in the 30C heat, and what could possibly go wrong? Answer: all sorts of things – but I couldn't tell you what they were, as I have no memory of that night at all. From what I was told later, I got so drunk I fell asleep – or I passed out – in a chair. Someone thought it would be a good idea to put both me and the chair into the swimming pool, a prank which, at the very least, would have woken me up with a start. I was lifted up and dropped into the pool, and people stood around watching, waiting to see my reaction. I assume they expected to see a shocked, wet, and probably very pissed-off Para splutter to the surface and threaten retribution while they all scarpered, laughing. So, they watched, and they waited.

The problem was, I didn't move, even when I was completely submerged. This clearly wasn't what they had in mind. If they had left me there, I would have drowned. Once the pranksters realised that was a very real possibility, they had to jump in to rescue me. They managed to fish me out of the water just in time, and I managed to avoid the embarrassment of surviving a land mine explosion in Afghanistan only to die in a tame tourist swimming pool in Oman.

At this point, when it looked as if my evening could not really get any worse, a guy from the embassy came over to pay the bill and I puked on his trousers, which he wasn't expecting. All in all, this was not my finest hour.

I was so pissed that when the 14-hour layover was up, they wouldn't allow me to get back onto the plane. To be fair, they did try to show lenience. I just had to prove I could walk in a straight line but, impressively, I completely failed the test. They also asked me to recite the alphabet backwards, but I would have struggled to say the letters in the right order, so that was beyond me. The result was I was barred from the plane and I missed my flight. I had to wait for the next one and, as expected, I got a right chewing from my sergeant for my behaviour, which only ended when he asked me, "Do you want a shell or a fine?"

The fine was going to be £150, and I wasn't having that. We didn't get much pay in the army and I didn't want to be broke just as I was going off on leave. So, I chose a shell. Let me explain. The Wombat recoilless, anti-tank weapon fires a 120mm shell which weighs 22kg. That last part is important, because punishment in the Parachute Regiment came in the form of tasks carried out with that bloody heavy thing on your shoulder. First, you had to wear full uniform, including smock and helmet. You picked up the shell and marched with it on your shoulder down to the commanding officer's base, because officially it was his punishment you were receiving. That punishment usually lasted 45 minutes but, if the sergeant thought you weren't working hard enough, it could go on for much longer. He would have you marking time in the cook house, then get you running up and down hills with the Wombat shell still on your shoulder. I'd done it once before, when I was punished for turning up on duty pissed, no use to man nor beast, so I knew I could handle a shelling.

There was another reason why I chose the shell – it had nothing to do with saving money. I would earn more respect from everyone, including the person dishing out the punishment. That day though, the choice was taken away from me. When I reported for my punishment, it turned out there was a ban on the shell because someone had collapsed during an earlier punishment session. That meant I had to pay the £150 fine after all. I was not happy!

CHAPTER 9

HERE WE GO AGAIN – IRAQ

I badly missed my family in prison, even though I had been used to being away from home for long stretches. This was not the first time I had been stuck in a foreign land without my loved ones around me, and that made the time a little easier to handle. But a posting in the armed forces was for a fixed duration – we knew when we were going to return home – and that was the exact opposite of the situation in Chennai. There, the authorities told us almost nothing, and we had no clue how long we would be held for.

At the back end of 2009, I was sent to Iraq with 1 Para for a tour that stretched through the winter till the following April. That meant I would be spending Christmas far away from my family. That was a painful wrench, but I had volunteered to join up, and no-one was forcing me to be in the regiment. I also knew it would be for a set time, a number of months that I could count and tolerate because, at the end of it, I would definitely be able to go on leave and see everyone again. I could deal with most things if I knew the experience was going to end after a while. One of the worst parts of being banged up in Chennai was the uncertainty, never knowing from one day to the next when there would be a new twist in the saga, and what that might mean. Would a politician make a breakthrough on our behalf? Would our lawyer come up with something that might get us released? Would it make any difference anyway, if the authorities simply chose to ignore them all and keep us locked up forever to make their point?

At least in Iraq there was a system in place that I could understand and relate to. There was a chain of command and rules of engagement. I had a job to do and a role to perform that I had been well trained for. Of course, there was also the ever-present danger of snipers and improvised explosive devices (IEDs), but we all knew that came with the territory. We accepted the risk.

I spent Christmas Day 2009 in an alleyway in Iraq, keeping an eye out for trouble. I was there all day from 10am to 10pm, and it was a complete waste of time. Nothing happened that day, but we had to be there, so moaning about it was pointless. We finally got some dinner around midnight and ended up celebrating Christmas on Boxing Day. Somehow, it went downhill and ended up as a massive food fight, which only broke up when one bloke got lamped over the head with a television. We had to stop before it got completely out of hand, but it was quite fun as I recall.

In Iraq, we were always looking out for signs of danger. The threat from snipers and IEDs was very real, even in the city. Insurgents didn't care about civilian deaths. They would blow us up no matter the cost. If they could kill or maim coalition forces, they would go ahead and act without hesitation, even if they killed a bunch of bystanders in the process.

In prison, that sixth sense for danger was always primed. We had to watch our backs and keep an eye out for anyone who might be looking to start trouble. There was nearly always somebody who wanted to attack us or mess us up. That was probably less stressful for me than for an average civilian because I could handle myself. I was used to living with danger close by. I'd been trained with that mindset in the army – to be alert and spot a potential threat before it became real. That was a skill I hadn't lost, and it had been honed to a sharp edge in two war zones. In the end, that mentality had become second nature.

In Iraq, we had to be in a constant state of alert. When we drove around, cars would drift close to our vehicles, and we would have to show the drivers our weapons so they could see we meant business and know to back off. We travelled around in bulky Bushmasters, and I was often the driver. The Bushmaster was an Aussie-made, four-wheel-drive, armoured vehicle that we suped-up. They had protruding horns on the front that were designed to trigger tripwires for IEDs. That made the Bushmaster look like an angry bull, so we were pretty distinctive out on the streets.

When we were out of the vehicles and on the ground in urban areas, we were very exposed. We would be surrounded by high windows and rooftops, and any one of them could have easily housed a sniper. There wasn't much we could do about that possibility. I didn't worry about it exactly, but it was always there, playing on my mind.

Our time could be filled with variety as well as boredom. One day, we were sent to a police compound that was being used to house cars that once belonged to Saddam Hussein's notorious eldest son, Uday, who was killed by coalition forces in 2003. The guy was infamous for doing whatever he liked while his father was president, including murder, torture and rape. He had accumulated a lot of wealth and was said to have owned hundreds of luxury cars, including a Ferrari F40, Porsches, BMWs, and a variety of Rolls Royces and Bentleys. We had stumbled on a few of the psychopath's collection, and it was a surreal moment to see all of these luxury cars lined up in that compound. They were still sitting there, long after their owner had been killed, gathering dust because no-one knew what to do with them.

We also got to see a mix of places around Iraq because we were often the back-up boys, responsible for the security of other people's meetings, whether they were politicians or army top brass. One meeting was held in a palace. On another job, we had to go to a hospital. There were a few Iraqis outside, just standing around in the street, eating. They were friendly enough, and I was offered some of their food. It looked all right, so I thought I'd give it a go. My mates were saying, "What are you doing? You don't even know what it is. It could be anything." They were right – but I was hungry, and these people had offered to share their meal with me. I took some and ate it, much to the amazement of the lads who were looking on. It was OK too and, for the record, I think it was boiled goat, but I couldn't exactly be sure.

There has been a lot of crap written in the British press about the American military having a low opinion of British forces following our joint ops in Afghanistan and Iraq but, honestly, we were better soldiers than they were. They reckoned we were under-equipped, and maybe we were, especially compared to the enormous US war machine which never seemed to run out of anything. The Americans were never short of gear and nearly always had something to trade that we considered "Gucci". That was our word for a particularly nice bit of kit that was normally out of our reach, unless we traded. I was amazed by the US soldiers' attitude to their own gear. They placed so little value on what they had in their possession. I offered one a regimental top, and he was so excited to get hold of something with a British Para insignia on it, he offered me all sorts of riches in return. When we got something Gucci, we really appreciated it. The US Rangers would give us windproof jackets or a GPS worth a hundred quid in exchange for a simple 'reg top'. They thought this was an awesome trade, and they had so much kit anyway, it didn't really matter. If the US army wanted to know where their equipment had gone, the soldiers would just lie and say, "It got broken." They'd be given another one, no questions asked. It was different for us. When I was deployed, I was given a personal GPS that, we were told, we could keep afterwards. At the end of the tour, we were ordered to hand them all over so they could be given to someone else.

It was the same in the bases. We used to go in their cook house and marvel at what the US soldiers were eating. We'd have steak and salmon when we ate with the US boys. Meanwhile, back in our own cook house, they'd be dishing up chips, beans and sausages again. Because their food was such a rare treat, we were really appreciative. The Americans just took their fine dining for granted.

Our store, the NAAFI, sold the basics only, so we would get the "jingly bus" – the old minibus that we were allowed to sign out – and head off to the Yanks' PX (exchange) store on their base. They had everything. I even managed to buy myself an iPod. It was a different world.

The media back home used to make it sound as if the US army thought we were clueless but, if anything, it was the other way around. We used to say that Americans had "all the gear but no idea". I'm excluding the Special Forces guys we met, obviously. The blokes in Delta Force and the Navy Seals were the elite, and the very best at what they did. They were worthy of anyone's respect. We used to get compared to the US airborne divisions, like the famous 101st, known as the "Screaming Eagles", but I reckon we were way better. We were more like the US Rangers. They worked with Delta Force and the Seals and, like us, they were a Special Forces Support Group. I rated them highly.

When it came to the average American soldier though, I was not impressed. I saw a lot of these "grunts" in Iraq and many didn't even look like soldiers. I'd see spotty kids who looked like they'd come straight out of high school. It was either that or the other extreme and they were too bulky. I'm into training and body-building, but some of these guys seemed too large to do the job. I would look at these very huge, muscly guys walking around and think, "You won't be on your feet for long in this heat." While the Brits would patrol on foot a lot of the time, the Yanks tended to stay in their vehicles until the moment they were needed. They were spoiled. They had all the nice food and all the fancy gear, but even the muscle-bound ones were not very effective as a fighting force. And they drank Gatorade like it was going out of fashion.

We got on all right though, and it helped that Americans seemed to love the British. That had always been true in civilian life, and I found it was the same in the military. American soldiers almost always liked their Brit counterparts. I had to visit the dentist while I was in Iraq, so I went to the nearest one on the US base. I walked in and was greeted by a bonny lass. When I opened my mouth to say something, she said, "Goddamn it, you're British. I love the British!" You don't normally get a welcome like that at the dentist!

Looking back, I'd agree that Saddam Hussein was an evil tyrant, and nobody mourned him or his sons, but there was a massive downside to deposing him. Without him, there was no order. That fall-out was what we were called in to remedy. Cities in Iraq used to be well looked-after, but the ones I saw were shit-holes, and dangerous shit-holes at that. After we stuck our oar in, the whole country turned to shit. It doesn't matter how we justified why we went to war – to avenge the 9/11 atrocity; to make the world a safer place; or to remove Saddam and his non-existent weapons of mass destruction – in the end, it was all about oil. And, as for making Iraq safer, well, hundreds of thousands of civilians died there after Saddam was killed.

We could never fully relax in Iraq, and we had to stay professional despite the distractions because there was always the possibility of a sniper or an IED with our name on it. But, in truth, it was a lot calmer during our deployment than it had been in previous years, and I was lucky that things weren't as bad as they could have been. Thankfully, we managed to get to the end of our tour with no casualties, and every one of us came safely home.

CHAPTER 10

TIME FOR A CHANGE

When I got back from Iraq, in March 2010, I was hoping for a better posting. We were supposed to head off to Belize next, and that was a really promising prospect. We needed jungle training if we were going to continue to support Special Forces, who could be deployed anywhere in the world at short notice. Besides, we deserved a rewarding tour after we had been posted to the hell-holes of Afghanistan and Iraq.

I couldn't believe it when we were told we wouldn't be going to Belize after all. Two companies before us had gone out there for six weeks each. I was with A Company by now, and we were told there was nothing left in the budget. Instead, we would be going off to Sennybridge Training Area in Powys, Wales. No offence to the Welsh, but it was not quite the same!

We were gutted at missing out. How could there be no funding for training for the Special Forces Support Group? The army had to be joking. I was really deflated because I would have loved to have trained in a jungle environment. I began to sense the decision was political, and my suspicions only grew when we found out later that the company directly after us had also gone to Belize.

Now that I was back in the UK, I realised I had a decision to make about my future. As a young man, all I had wanted to be was a Para and, once I was in the regiment, I put all of my energy into my training, making sure I was able to do the job to the best of my ability without letting anyone down. I had survived being blown up in Afghanistan and made it through my tour of Iraq without a scratch. I was almost 24 years old, and I was thinking – what now?

There was the possibility of returning to Iraq for another tour, but my thought was – been there, done that, and had the campaign medals to prove it. In the Paras, we were expected to be sent into trouble spots and war zones, but often that meant more of the same. For the first time, I began to question whether army life was what I really wanted. What was the point of repeating the same experiences over and over again?

Times change, and friends I'd known for years were starting to leave. I knew some guys who had taken up resettlement courses provided by the army, so I knew how that worked. We would get a healthy grant to help get us back into civilian life, and that sounded pretty good to me. I had served for six years in the Paras. Sometimes I wish I had stayed on longer, but I had definitely come to a turning point and needed a change. I had joined the Paras in 2004 and spent six months in Northern Ireland the following year. I was in Afghanistan in 2007 and 2008, then in Iraq in 2009 and 2010. I left the same year.

I was lucky. I never had any flashbacks from the time I was blown up in Afghanistan, nor did I suffer from post-traumatic stress disorder (PTSD) because of anything I had seen or done.

It wasn't trauma or disillusionment that prompted me to leave the Parachute Regiment. I just felt the time was right to move on and try something new. I will always be incredibly proud of being a Para, and I could not have received better support from the Regimental Association or the Army Benevolent Fund while I was in Chennai.

Money was also a factor in my decision. I was crap with it. In the army, I learned to get everything on tick. I lived like a pop star for a while then, when I ran out of cash, I lived off rations until I was paid again. It was naivety, I suppose, but I was just a lad and that's how we were. I used to think money was there to fund what I wanted when I wanted it, so I made sure I always spent the "Queen's paper", as we called it. Now I was older and wiser, I understood that I had to put money aside and save for the better things in life. I guess it was all part of growing up.

So I knew I wanted out, and I felt like I should be earning better money than an enlisted man, but what could I do if I moved into civilian life? I was a soldier, and that's all I had been trained to be from the age of 18. I had a specific set of skills to sell to the private sector and, although the opportunities were few and far between, I had heard blokes like me were making good money from close protection work. I fancied a bit of that.

Once I told the regiment I wanted to leave, I was dealt with fairly. I went on extended leave until I received a phone call telling me I needed to come down to St Athan and finish the paperwork before I was officially out. After a few weeks off, I returned to my unit. I was given a room to myself in barracks, and I went through the process of handing back my military kit in order to get the stamps that would show I had done everything that was asked of me, and there was no equipment still in my possession.

This all became a bit of a nark. I had to go to various different places on the base to hand in my kit and get each stamp, all in the right order. It was tricky, because I was supposed to be in uniform, and I was also meant to hand in that uniform. I could hardly walk round the base naked!

Finally, I managed to get all my stamps, but I still had to find one last officer. I had a five-hour journey ahead of me to get home, it was a Friday afternoon, and there was hardly anyone around, including the officer. Finally, he turned up at 4pm. I said, "Boss, is there any chance you can just sign this?" He asked me why I was leaving. I kept my answers short and to the point because I didn't want an exit interview. My time with the regiment was up, and I didn't want a fuss. I just wanted to be out of there. He signed my form and that was me done.

It was a strange feeling to leave there after six years in the Paras. Military life was all I had known since leaving school. A lot had happened to me in my time with the regiment. I'd been to Northern Ireland, Afghanistan and Iraq. I'd grown up and been blown up. I was a very different person from the green 18-year-old who first went down to Catterick. I walked out of the base knowing I'd served my time, and I was a free man. I had the clothes that I travelled in, but not much else. The only signs I had to show I'd been a Para were the tattoos on my arms.

It was a long journey up to Newcastle and the train was delayed. When it finally pulled into York, I found out that the last connecting train had already left, and I was stranded there in the station for the night. There were no trains again till 6am the next morning. My first night out of the regiment, and I was forced to kip on a bench. Welcome to civilian life, I thought.

CHAPTER 11

LISA'S STORY: MY LITTLE BROTHER

My brother and I have always been close. I was seven years old when Nick was born, and I can still remember seeing him for the first time. Our mam was in the hospital for a couple of days, so I went in to see the new baby with my older brother Paul. I was so excited. I thought our new arrival was amazing. I couldn't wait to help mam look after him.

When we got the new baby home, mam had to watch me like a hawk. Whenever her back was turned, I was always trying to pick him up. She would shout, "No! Put the baby down Lisa!" I just wanted to hold him, and she was worried I would drop him. Mam let me cuddle him though, and I wanted to get involved in everything, including dressing him and changing nappies. I loved feeding him. If the baby was asleep, and I wanted some time with him, I would try to wake him up. I was only eight and didn't understand that I should be leaving him in peace. I suppose I thought he was like one of my dolls, but better, because he was real!

Our Paul is older than me, and there are 10 years between him and Nick. Paul looked after both of us, because he was our big brother, and, in turn, I looked after Nick. The gap in our ages meant I have always taken on a motherly role with him, even though my mam was there as well.

Nick was definitely spoilt when he was little, but that was my fault not his – I was the one doing the spoiling. When he was small, if he was "getting wrong" off my mam and dad, he would run upstairs and come crying to me. More often than not, I would tell him it was OK, he was a good boy, and he wasn't really being naughty. My mam and dad would overhear this and say, "You're spoiling him Lisa." They'd tell me it would be all my fault if he never learned how to behave. He turned out pretty well in the end though, so I don't think me spoiling Nick did any harm in the long run.

We were always close but, of course, being my little brother, he could also be an annoying little shit. He was the kind of boy who would pull the heads off my Barbie dolls if he didn't get his own way. But we still got on most of the time.

I work in the police control room. I take calls from members of families who are always reporting each other for something trivial. There are so many different family dynamics out there, and it makes me realise that we are a united and strong family compared to many.

Dad was a miner. Later he became a pipe liner. He instilled an old-fashioned work ethic in all of us. Both my parents worked, so we were pretty self-sufficient after school. Paul and I went to the same school, so we would be responsible for Nick when we came home. Paul was supposed to be the most responsible one, but I reckoned that was really my job.

When Nick was a little older, he became a classic stroppy teenager. He wasn't always grumpy, and he had a sense of humour, but at school he wasn't interested, and he really didn't apply himself. He couldn't cope with teachers telling him what to do and he was like that at home, too. He expected things to be done for him, and he never lifted a finger. Nick was very headstrong. You could nag him all you liked, but it wouldn't make any difference. You could try to tell him what to do, but he would be the one who decided if he wanted to do it. When he first told us that he wanted to join the army, we were convinced that overcoming this attitude would be his biggest hurdle. We'd say to him, "How on earth are you going to cope with being ordered around by a sergeant when you won't be told what to do by a teacher or anyone else?" He'd just say, "Well, I want to be there."

Then we'd ask him how he would manage to do all the chores when he couldn't even make his bed. He'd tell us firmly, "It will be different."

I don't think we ever truly doubted him though. We knew he had it in him. He just needed to care enough and, ultimately, he proved to everyone that he did.

I didn't know much about the Paras before he joined up, apart from the fact that they jumped out of planes. I laughed at the thought of Nick trying that. I assumed he would eventually go off and do something else instead: he'd either give up the idea of the army altogether or end up as a Fusilier. I really couldn't see him jumping out of planes. Looking back though, dad used to get him those toy soldiers, the ones with parachutes attached with string. He'd throw them up in the air and watch them float back down again. So, really, it's all dad's fault!

I always felt very protective of Nick, and that certainly didn't change when he went off to join the army. I had mixed feelings at the time. I was glad he had found something he wanted to do, but I was a bit apprehensive as well. Nick wasn't a big lad, after all. He was short and not muscly like he is now. I was worried he was going to be bullied. I wondered how he would adapt to military life and fit in with everybody. As for the selection test, if he failed, I certainly wouldn't have viewed him as a failure, so I didn't think it mattered very much to us. I never considered he might have needed to pass for a deeper reason. I only realised later that Nick might have been trying to prove a point, not to our family, but to himself.

Not that he had anything to prove to us at all. We were just proud that he wanted to do something worthwhile with his life. He could have been in the army band, or one of the cooks, we would have been just as proud.

At the beginning, my mam and I were naïve about what Nick had actually signed up for. When I thought about him going through the selection process, I really didn't have a clue what he was up to. I just assumed he would be down at Catterick with a compass, outdoors somewhere, orienteering through a field or forest. If I had known about "milling" and him being punched, I'd have been horrified. When I watched a video showing Nick and the other candidates in training, it hit me. This was real. He was playing with the big boys now.

I didn't quite appreciate how special the Paras were until we went to the passing out parade. Seeing him and all the others in their uniforms on that parade ground, then watching the videos the regiment showed us about its history and heritage, that's when it dawned on me. Nick's achievement in becoming a Para was massive. I felt nothing but pure pride. The older guys from the regiment were there on that day too, as well as veterans from previous generations, so I could put Nick's amazing achievement into some kind of context. It was just an incredible day.

When I think about what the Paras do – the way they throw themselves out of aeroplanes – I think they're nuts. That's why Nick fitted in so well. He's nuts too. He is not bothered about anything, and nothing fazes him. He told me about the night jump when he started spinning and was out of control with no time to properly correct the lines, so he just had to accept a hard landing. I thought, what the hell is he doing? One wrong move and he could have been killed. It really struck home.

The danger Nick faced was always at the back of our minds, especially when he was sent to Afghanistan. We constantly worried about him. I'd watch horror stories on the news about British soldiers being killed or wounded, and I would wonder, how did that affect Nick? Was he near that spot? Did he know the man who has been killed? At one point, there was a number of Paras killed or injured in a short space of time, and that was just unbearable.

Despite our worries, we never would have demanded that Nick leave just because we couldn't cope with the worry. Nick was headstrong, so he wouldn't have listened anyway. He was determined. He wanted this, and he was prepared to go out and do it, so we just had to accept his decision.

I was on holiday in Ibiza when Nick was blown up in Afghanistan. I knew nothing about it at first, which was probably just as well. My dad picked me up from the airport at the end of my holiday and the first thing I said to him was, "How's Nick?" I'd only been away a week, but I had to know straight away that my brother was OK. My dad was pushing the luggage trolley and said, "He's all right." Then he said, quite calmly, "He got blown up but he's OK."

"Blown up! You what?"

I'll never forget that moment. I'm in the middle of Newcastle airport, and I'm going into one. "Blown up? What are you on about, dad? What happened?" I became so animated that my dad started laughing. That made me even more flustered.

Dad was only amused because he knew Nick was fine. He was as relieved as I was. "Calm down," he said. "He's all right." Then he said, "The Land Rover, though, is not all right." And he laughed about that too.

"The Land Rover? I don't care about the bloody Land Rover!"

That was dad. There were loads of times in the coming years, while Nick was stuck in India and I was at my worst, when I'd be stressed and manic, and I would start ranting, not pausing to draw a breath, and dad would start laughing and say, "You need to chill out, Lisa."

When Nick came home from Afghanistan, we were relieved, but then he was sent to Iraq and the worrying inevitably started all over again. Nick didn't tell me much about what he was getting up to over there and, frankly, I didn't want to know. I just knew he was doing serious stuff with serious people. All I could hope was that somehow my little brother would be OK.

After all that worry, when Nick told us he was thinking of leaving the Paras, I was hugely relieved. I certainly wasn't going to talk him out of his decision. He had served his country, and I am incredibly proud of my brother for that, but I quickly saw the upside. If he left the army, it would give us all a break from the constant worry. Of course, when I look back now, nothing could have been further from the truth, but none of us knew then that he would face greater trials in civilian life, and our worries would be so much greater. At the time, I just remember thinking that he'd be out of danger, he would get a normal, sensible job, and this would turn out great for everyone. He had picked up skills in the Parachute Regiment that would serve him for life.

I don't know why exactly Nick decided to leave the army, but I do remember that he went to a funeral of one of the men he knew and served with, and I think that affected him. He might not acknowledge the impact, but it seemed to shake him up at the time. Nick wears his heart on his sleeve, but he doesn't tell us everything, partly to protect us and prevent us from worrying. When he did discuss the dangers he faced – such as the time he was blown up – he hides behind humour and makes light of it. But I was concerned he might be bottling it all up, storing trouble for later. He gradually started to think differently about army life, and maybe he started to have reservations – but Paras aren't supposed to have feelings, are they? It is a very manly world. Paras tend to act the way they think they are supposed to. But they do have feelings, and they have families to care about. I don't think it's possible to live that kind of life, facing all those dangers on a daily basis, without being affected by it.

Society has changed a lot since Nick was arrested in India. Now, it is not only OK to talk about men and mental health, it is very prominent as an issue. People are not as judgmental as they were. Back when Nick was part of that world, men didn't speak about their feelings as much as they do now.

We did press Nick on his decision – asking him if he was sure about coming out of the military, and whether he was OK to leave the security of army life behind – but I was glad he didn't change his mind. He was young and could start again. He would never stop me from doing what I wanted to do, and I would never interfere in his life. To be honest, I couldn't really see a downside. Surely our days of worrying were over.

CHAPTER 12

CLOSE PROTECTION

When I have too much time on my hands, I tend to overthink things – and there was always too much time in prison. The days dragged and the nights were even worse, leaving my mind to churn things over. I ended up reliving every step that led me to where I was. My life seemed to be full of what-ifs. What if I had stayed in the Paras? What if I had just taken some boring security job? What if I'd put together enough money to go into the work I really wanted to do, instead of pursuing a shortcut into anti-piracy jobs?

In the private sector, my specialist skills were niche. I was interested in close protection at first. Businessmen and celebrities, even buildings, needed protecting, and my training meant I was an ideal fit. It wasn't just a case of being some big, tough bloke, like a nightclub bouncer, who could use their muscles to block anyone reaching a client. The job was far more complex and required greater brain power than that. I would have to be constantly appraising my surroundings, making sure I spotted a potential threat before it arose. I could relate to that mindset because that's what it felt like to be in a hostile environment. We always had to be at a high state of alert, able to visualise how and when trouble might arise.

The money for close protection could be good too. If I chose to work outside of the UK, the pay could get seriously tempting. A lot of people wouldn't like the idea of working in a war zone, but I knew it wouldn't bother me, particularly if there was the added attraction of a serious wedge of money at the end of it.

So, close protection seemed to be the obvious choice after I left the army. But there was one big problem. I couldn't afford it. I really fancied the work, and I knew I'd be good at it, but I couldn't just sign up to be someone's bodyguard without proper training. During my time in prison, as I faced day after endless day there, I played it all over in my mind. If I had just done the close protection course as soon as I had left the Paras, I wouldn't be in this bloody mess. That was a bitter realisation.

The main problem was money. Unfortunately, I didn't have any, and the course cost £3,000. I didn't have anywhere near enough saved at that point. That lack of cash was the main factor that propelled me down a different route, one which ended up with me languishing in prison in India.

Immediately after I left the Paras, I took on routine security jobs. It was boring work compared to my previous life in the regiment. I was just keeping an eye on buildings. To be honest, it drove me mad. The biggest adjustment was the change of pace. I was used to getting things done, and done fast, with no bullshit. In civilian life, I was working at a far slower pace. Any time I tried to get anything sorted, I was told it couldn't be done, and I would have to wait. I'd think, why? For two years, I tried to get used to this rhythm of life and the civilian way of doing things, but I found it really difficult to adjust.

I was on low pay doing the basic security work, and it was bloody boring. Worse still, I was trapped. I couldn't afford to take the course I needed, and I wasn't being paid enough to put any money aside. Close protection was still my main goal, but how the hell was I going to achieve it, stuck in a rut like this?

The money in close protection was good and there was stability, but there were other obstacles too. Even if I passed the course, I knew it would be hard for me to secure that kind of work in the face of stiff competition. I'd be starting from scratch. No-one would know me or what I could do. It was the age-old problem of needing experience to get jobs, but how could I gain experience without any work? I would need time and contacts to get a break.

It was that frustrating combination of circumstances that led me to make what turned out to be a fateful decision. I decided to take a maritime course. It would still cost a few quid, but it was cheaper than close protection training and, back then, I was likely to get straight onto a job. The course itself only cost a few hundred pounds, which I could just about scrape together, and once I was qualified, I'd make the money back.

There was a big demand for men like me caused by the increased threat of piracy. When I first heard that guys were getting paid to protect ships from pirates, I thought it was a joke. I mean, pirates? In the 21st century? It seemed like a crazy idea. But the more I learned, the more I understood. An entire industry had sprung up to combat this very real and modern threat. Somali pirates were making millions hijacking ships in the Indian Ocean then ransoming the vessels, cargo and crews back to the owners. This had been going for over a decade and was costing an estimated $6 billion a year. Ship owners had decided it was a lot cheaper to hire former servicemen like myself to guard their precious vessels than to leave everything to chance.

The money was good too. As a Para, I earned £18,000 a year but, on the ships, I could make $5,000 a month, or £3,800, tax-free. If I worked without a break, I'd be clearing £45,000 a year – or two and a half times what I was earning in the army. The risk of attack wasn't even that great. With the training I'd received and the firepower we'd be carrying with us, I was confident we could deal with any threat from trigger-happy pirates. Besides, I'd heard they were nearly always high on khat, a plant-based stimulant like speed, which was bound to have a negative effect on their reasoning, as well as their aim.

A mate of mine recommended this line of work, and I decided to go for it. Years later, I saw him again, and he said he felt terrible he had been the one to put the idea into my head. I told him that no-one could have foreseen what would happen, and I certainly felt no ill-will towards the guy.

Once I had decided on my new career, the first stage was to go on an anti-piracy training course and earn my British Seaman's card. My plan was to send my CV to companies that provided former servicemen for maritime protection. It seemed like the right thing to do. I knew I couldn't carry on like I was. I was 25, and I wanted to start earning some proper money. Also, I was desperate to escape the boredom. I figured that anything was better than nine-to-five in an office or factory. This was too attractive an opportunity to ignore, so I signed up.

In September 2011, I rocked up to take my maritime course in, of all places, Stoke, which is landlocked. It soon became clear I wasn't the only one hoping to make a few bob out of my military experience – even though it was a stretch for some, who were clearly taking the piss. One guy on my course described himself as ex-military, but he had been out of the army for 20 years, working as a taxi driver, so his skills would have been a bit on the rusty side. With some of the other waifs and strays on the course I thought, you might have been in the army lads, but when was that? Back in the days of shields and swords?

The course was simple for someone who had completed training with the Paras. We had to display weapons competency and learn the correct operational procedures to carry out the work on board ship. It was nothing I couldn't pick up pretty easily.

Once I had finished my course, I did some more bog-standard security jobs on land while I waited for my first anti-piracy job. In the meantime, and with help from my mam, I managed to scrape together enough money to take a close protection course, which was still my ambition. I knew the course would be worth doing, and I couldn't break into that world without it. I had to learn vehicle drills and bodyguard duties, and the instructors set us up to deal with any hazardous situation we were likely to encounter. In realistic tests, we were shown what to do if we were travelling in two vehicles and were ambushed. The client could be in the lead vehicle which might have been disabled in a gunfight. So, I'd have to act fast and, while under assault from small arms fire, get the VIP to safety. The close protection drills for that scenario involved engaging the attackers, getting everyone into one vehicle, and driving away from the scene.

We were taught how to evaluate a location before the VIP arrived. So, for example, if there was a meeting in a restaurant, I would have to know where to park to make a rapid escape if that was necessary. I would have to know how to assess traffic flow outside, spot weak points, and clock the fire exit nearest to the table. I was trained how to keep a rowdy person at arm's length, using non-lethal force, or by using "soft skills", like talking the guy down. I didn't want to kill some pissed-up bloke who was just stumbling around the place if I could calm him down with a few words. We learnt a number of highly effective defensive and offensive techniques, and we were taught by a variety of people who knew exactly what they were doing. It was all useful stuff, and very different from the training I had been used to in the military.

Playing in the back of my mind was the thought that I could be sent back to Iraq in a close protection role. Maybe I'd be looking after the chief executive of some company with investments in the Middle East. But I consoled myself with the thought that I wouldn't be entirely in the danger zone and, besides, I would be making way more money than when I was there as a Para, so I wouldn't be risking my life every day for very little gain.

Despite completing all the courses that I needed, and spending time and money on my training, I never really got a break in close protection. Like I feared, it was hard getting into that world when the old sweats already in the business didn't know me. Despite all the training I had received and the new skills I had picked up along the way, I never did any close protection jobs. The business was heaving with military veterans, and there was just too much competition for me to gain a foothold.

It seemed there was less fierce competition in anti-piracy. I did a few transits on various ships, and I started to receive money, no problem. I took on more and more work from different maritime companies and went with the flow. I undertook a dozen jobs on different ships, and we were never once attacked by pirates.

It was easier to get work on the ships. That was how it was. I couldn't do anything about it, so I decided I would keep on doing it. But my decision to return to sea was going to have a massive effect on my life in ways I could never have imagined at the time.

I did think I would have another crack at close protection work at some stage – but that was all derailed by Chennai. Maritime security came knocking and I answered because it was a job I knew and liked. I was single, I was earning good money and meeting people of all nationalities. As a young man not long out of the military, I felt I was living like a pop star.

There was a lot of travel in between assignments, so I saw a fair amount of the world, which was always good, particularly when someone else was paying the fare. I visited South Africa, Kuwait, Jordan, Egypt and the Maldives, but I was only ever in each of those countries for a day or two while I waited for a job somewhere else.

I saw Sri Lanka the most, because that was the main hub for the anti-piracy work. There were always plenty of former Paras around, and I was always bumping into someone I knew. I was more than 5,000 miles from home, but suddenly I'd see a guy I'd served with at Catterick.

One of these encounters happened while I was out in Sri Lanka waiting for a job. I met someone I knew, and during our chat, he said, "Why you don't you come and work with us? You might have heard bad reports about the company, but it is all under control now." I knew the company he mentioned, and he was right, I had heard some stories. The company was AdvanFort, and the rumours I'd been hearing centred on the crap weapons they supplied to their men. Also, I'd heard people weren't getting paid on time – but that wasn't unusual. Loads of companies in the anti-piracy business were lax like that. It seemed to come with the territory. I had worked for a company which still owed me four grand, and I never got to see a penny, so it wasn't out of the ordinary. I was apprehensive but I figured I should take a chance.

The location of AdvanFort's anti-piracy recruitment section was the tipping point that convinced me to take a look. It was based in Newcastle, on the Quayside. The company had moved to the city because one of their top guys was a Geordie. It couldn't have been more convenient, and I was sick of travelling down south every time I wanted a job. I decided I would give AdvanFort a go.

When I turned up for the interview, in September 2013, I didn't look like a former Para. I had just landed back in the country. I had hair everywhere, a beard, and I was tanned. I was also wearing shorts and a vest as I hadn't had the time to get spruced up. I looked so weird that I was stopped by the curious border authorities at Newcastle Airport. They asked to see my passport, which I thought was strange since I was coming off an internal flight from London. To the border officials, I must have looked like a foreigner, and a dodgy one too. But, as soon as they heard my accent, they realised their mistake. I was definitely local – I just didn't look it.

At the interview, I apologised for not being at my neatest, explaining about my flight. The interviewers didn't seem to mind. They were more interested in ensuring I knew what I was doing. They asked me a few bog-standard maritime questions, and I knew all the answers, so they were satisfied. They just wanted to get my name on their books, and I happily obliged, signing on the dotted line.

That was another turning point in my life that I thought about a lot while I was in Chennai prison. I could have messed up or missed that interview. I could have been rejected because I was so dishevelled. I might have had second thoughts and decided to look elsewhere. But, on paper, we were a good fit. AdvanFort needed men like me, and their local connection made the company a very tempting option. It was easy. Too easy, as I was later to find out.

When I set off on my next job, everything suggested it would be like all the others I had under my belt. First, I flew to Kuwait and did another job to Sri Lanka. Then I went to Muscat in Oman and sailed back to Sri Lanka. There, I was told I would be boarding a ship owned by AdvanFort, transported by speedboat. That was when I first saw, and then boarded, the MV Seaman Guard Ohio, which was basically a floating armoury, with men on board waiting to be deployed onto other ships for anti-piracy operations. The vessel was 45 metres long and unmistakeable, even from a distance, because it had the words "Seaman Guard" written in huge red and black lettering down its side, set against a background of battleship grey. There were a load of antenna sticking up into the air above the cabin, which picked up an array of satellite navigational and comms signals.

I didn't know it then, of course, but when I next left the ship it would be straight into the hands of the Indian police, and I wouldn't see my home again for years.

CHAPTER 13

STITCHED UP

I boarded the MV Seaman Guard Ohio on 6 October 2013. The ship was anchored just off the coast of Sri Lanka at the time, in international waters. The company had a small RIB which it used to transport people to and from their security jobs on different vessels. I jumped on board and I was soon on my way.

There was nothing particularly unusual about that day. People were coming and going, and I was essentially a passenger until I was needed for a job on another ship, usually as part of a three-man team. But, for now, there was nothing to do but wait.

There were 35 of us on board. We were responsible for the weapons, all of which were legal and signed off with the right paperwork and certificates. There was little threat to shipping from pirates and we weren't operational, so our arsenal and kit were locked away. I didn't even have a sidearm. If there had been a threat to us, we would have been able to reach our weapons quickly but, for the time being, we didn't need them.

I knew I might be aboard that vessel for a week or two before I was given an op. Although that was likely to be boring, I was happy enough earning money for nothing. If my bosses wanted to pay me to sit on a boat, fishing, sunbathing and working out with my resistance bands, then that was just fine. So what if I was stuck on a boat in the middle of the ocean? There were worse ways to earn a living.

One of the lads had the chance to leave our boat and take on a job at short notice. He didn't pursue the offer. For whatever reason, he chose to stay on board the Seaman Guard Ohio and let another guy take his place instead. That turned out to be a terrible mistake. It meant he was still there when the coastguard boarded us and took us into port. About seven or eight other guys did disembark just before we were apprehended, and his ordeal must have been made even worse, knowing that he didn't leave when he had the chance. That decision cost him years of freedom.

I'm not obsessed with the idea of bad luck but, looking back on it, we had another big chunk just after I went on board – and it led directly to our arrest. The company had arranged for a vessel to supply us with the fuel, food and water. Because we were around 40 nautical miles out to sea at this point, the crew of the supply vessel refused to make the entire journey. Instead, they wanted us to move closer towards land and meet them halfway.

The fishermen weren't being entirely lazy. They knew they shouldn't be transporting fuel on a small ship like theirs, and they must have known they were breaking the law. Not surprisingly, they wanted to minimise the risk of getting caught.

It took about two hours for them to do around 40 nautical miles, and the size of their vessel meant the crew would need two, or even three, journeys just to transport the fuel. Add in more journeys to load food and water, and it was likely to be a long night.

The weather didn't help either. There was a cyclone in the area. It was quite a distance away from us, but the tail-end of it was still making the sea choppy. This was another reason the fishermen said we should wait closer to the shore – their small vessel didn't want to be moving fuel in rough seas. The cyclone did provide some legal cover for us though because, under maritime law, we were permitted to move away from danger if conditions were potentially hazardous to our boat.

Either way, and without us knowing anything about it, the captain made the fateful decision to move us into Indian territorial waters during the night while most of us were sleeping. Regardless of the circumstances of the decision, I must stress we were allowed to be there, and there was never any intention to dock in an Indian port.

The water was looking very choppy when our crew started to bring large fuel barrels over by rope from the vessel alongside. This all looked very dodgy to me. There should have been a pipe which connected to a hose, so fuel could pour directly into the ship's tank. Instead, our fuel was being delivered by barrels which were strapped to this little, motorised fishing vessel. The barrels were then levered aboard using ropes and pulleys. This was not the way it should have been done.

The only act of wrongdoing that was ever committed during this whole saga was what was happening now: the way the fishermen brought that fuel out to us and then hoisted it onto the Seaman Guard Ohio. Their vessel wasn't fit for purpose and certainly not equipped to carry fuel in that way.

What happened to those fishermen was a classic example of the way things worked in India, and how the justice system could be manipulated to suit the agenda of whoever was in charge. We were detained, but the fishermen weren't arrested, let alone prosecuted. They were let off because nobody in charge gave a damn about whether they were convicted or not. They had bigger fish to fry – and that was us.

I went off to bed that night and fell asleep, totally unaware that my life would soon be completely derailed by the next day's events.

When I woke the next morning, 12 October 2013, Paul Towers told me that we were being boarded by the Indian coastguard from the coastal patrol vessel ICGS Naiki Devi. Paul told us that the coastguard official was armed, and he had ordered us to head for the port of Tuticorin in the Indian state of Tamil Nadu. At that point, I was surprised but not too alarmed. This was India after all, a nation that was supposedly friendly to the UK and still a part of the Commonwealth. It was not as though we had been boarded by forces from Iran or some tinpot dictatorship. I didn't think anything bad was likely to happen.

The coastguard claimed we were in India's territorial waters, but we found out the port radar wasn't working, so how did they know where we were? Later, they changed their story further, telling anybody that would listen that they had "intercepted" us, but that wasn't true. We weren't even moving. They implied we were on our way somewhere and up to no good when they caught up with us. The truth was the Seaman Guard Ohio was stationary, with an anchor down, and we weren't doing anything or going anywhere. Some commentators said afterwards we should have informed the port authorities of any intentions of activity in their waters, but we had no such intentions. All we wanted to do was get our fuel and supplies then move on again.

We were also told later that someone had made a fateful mobile call before we were boarded which might have played a crucial part in all that followed. Apparently, he rang port side to speak to a representative of AdvanFort to complain he had not been paid. He wanted to make arrangements to leave the vessel. We don't know exactly what was said, but we heard rumours later that, at one point, he stated, "They have weapons." We think the police might have intercepted the call and overheard what he had to say.

The coastguard circled our boat, with a mounted machine gun pointed at us the whole time. The guy who had boarded us stood on the bridge watching us intently as we headed to port, acting as if he expected us to suddenly make a break for it.

The journey was a strange one. We motored into Tuticorin incredibly slowly, following the coastguard vessel at about two knots. We realised later our lack of speed was for the benefit of the authorities. The Port Authority was in the process of putting together a big welcoming committee for us, and we had to wait for the VIPs to assemble. The whole thing was a set-up.

The sun was shining as we chugged into port, and we spotted a sizeable crowd on the harbour. They had stage-managed a media event to show off their trophies. There were more than 50 people watching, and they all seemed to know what was going on, even though we still hadn't got a clue. Some of these people had travelled down from Mumbai, 800 miles away, so they must have received a tip-off that something big was about to happen, and they should make great efforts to be there. We couldn't work out who they all were, but we realised there were elements of the maritime police or Indian naval authorities present.

When we arrived in port, we were met by local uniformed police and members of Q Branch, the Criminal Investigations Division of the Tamil Nadu Police. There were some serious people in attendance, and they had probably been told to expect a showpiece arrest of mercenaries or gun runners, at the very least. Maybe they were even expecting to witness the removal of a hefty cache of drugs.

When the authorities who had travelled from Mumbai saw our papers, they realised we were completely legit. At that point, none of them wanted to know. They knew there was no crime and nothing to concern them. The local, uniformed police had wasted their time, and now Q Branch CID guys were going to end up with egg on their faces. The coastguard had hauled in an innocent crew for no reason, and it appeared they'd dragged high-ranking officials all the way down from Mumbai for something and nothing. At this point, the local police should have admitted we had done nothing wrong, and we should have been allowed to leave. But apparently, no way were Q Branch officers going to allow themselves to look foolish, even if it meant jailing innocent men.

To save face, Q Branch officers decided to claim that our weapons were illegal. There was no evidence to support this bizarre allegation, and we sensed they didn't really believe it themselves.

We were one of many legitimate anti-piracy operations protecting international shipping, and we had all of the necessary certificates for our guns, which were safely locked away. Among the weapons in our arsenal on board the ship were six Heckler and Koch G3 machine guns. These had been adapted to ensure they could only fire semi-automatically, in compliance with maritime law. There was no way to convert these weapons back to automatic firing, which would have made them illegal. We had certificates proving all this. The guns had even been transported through India before they reached us! None of that mattered. Q Branch wanted us to be guilty and that was that. They ignored all our explanations and paperwork. This was when we first recognised a trait that would become a regular feature of our future lives – Q Branch officers were never going to allow little things like truth, facts or evidence get in the way of the convictions they were now seeking.

If Q Branch officers really did believe we had illegal weapons on board, they had a strange way of handling the situation. Surely, in those circumstances, they would have moved pretty quickly to remove these allegedly illegal guns from the ship. We were still on board, with full access to the armoury. If we really were the desperate and hardened criminals that they made us out to be, we could have easily made a stand. Instead, officers waited four days to remove these dangerous, supposedly illegal, weapons from our possession. Again, they made a big show of it when they finally did decide to come down and retrieve this crucial evidence. In fact, they went way over the top. They turned up mob-handed in a massive DAF truck which had to be at least a four tonner, with

30 armed men in the back. Ridiculous. We had no intention of resisting. We had been totally open about the guns, and they were still under lock and key, just like we said they were. We weren't hiding anything.

When we first got into port on the 12 October, we had decided the best course of action was for us to stay on board until this mess was sorted out. None of us wanted to leave the ship, so we spent six days aboard in port before the police moved in. That gave us enough time to contact our families and let them know what was going on. That was important for a number of reasons, not least because stories had started to appear in the media. Even at that stage, the distortions were getting into print, with some reporters claiming we had been picked up for gun running. I spoke to dad. He said he needed to know the truth, and he wanted to hear it from me. He asked me outright if we were running guns. I said, "No! Don't be fucking stupid. Our paperwork is all in order for the guns. Hopefully it will all be resolved soon." That seemed to reassure him that I hadn't done anything stupid or been caught up in any activity that was likely to land me in serious trouble. At this point, we were all still hoping everything would work out fine, and we would soon be on our way.

After several days confined to the boat, doubts about our prospects started to creep in. We ended up staying on the ship until 18 October, all the time waiting for the police to make their move. When they finally took action, they used a technique that was another feature of all our future dealings: they lied, blatantly, and to our faces.

On the morning of 18 October, officers said they wanted us to leave the ship. When we asked them why, they said, "You are going off to the hospital now." No-one believed a word of it. When we questioned why a large group of healthy blokes needed to visit hospital, we were told doctors were going to check us over to make sure we were free of disease. This sounded ridiculous, particularly as we hadn't even set foot on Indian soil. We had remained on board the whole time we were in port. Any lingering doubts we had about their true intentions soon evaporated when they told us, "You can't take reading glasses or cigarettes and you can't wear a belt." What kind of hospital was this? It sounded a lot like the rules of a police station or prison. We knew now for sure we were in serious trouble.

That was the day my life changed forever. We realised our stand-off couldn't carry on indefinitely. The police had a choice: they were either going to have to let us go, or they would have to intervene. We suspected the second course of action was more likely, especially when we discovered British Consular officials had been banned from seeing us. That made us even more suspicious.

We knew we were going to be arrested. We were told we could make phone calls home, and I knew this one was going to be difficult, but important. It could be the last call I would be allowed for a while. I knew I had to speak to Lisa, sharpish, so I could tell her what had to be done to get me out of this mess. Once again, my luck deserted me. It was 4am back home in Ashington when I phoned, and Lisa was asleep. I didn't have any choice. I had to phone my mam so I could tell someone in the UK first-hand what was happening. When she picked up the phone, I said. "Mam, it's all going to rat-shit now. They are removing us from the vessel, and we are going to be arrested. I don't know when I will next get to see or speak to you, but I love you and please don't worry about me. I'll be OK."

I didn't want mam to fret, but I had no option. Understandably she was frantic, so I spent most of the call reassuring her and saying that she shouldn't stress about me, even though I knew she would. I felt bad that I had somehow put myself in this situation, even though I had done nothing wrong. I didn't know it at the time, but that was the last normal conversation I would ever have with my mam. I still carry such a lot of guilt at causing her so much pain.

By now, Lisa was awake, and she had realised she had missed my call. I rang her back. There was no time left for a long discussion, soppiness or emotion. I had to get straight to the point. "Lisa, we are being arrested. Get on to the embassy now and get them to come down here. I love you and I will speak to you when I can."

We had to comply with the police demands to leave the ship otherwise we would have been forcibly removed, and the situation could have turned violent. I reckon we could have inflicted some serious damage on any raiding party, but it would have only played into their hands. We would have been the ones to suffer in the long run. They were desperate to demonstrate we were criminals, so acts of violence would only hinder our chances of being released, giving them just the proof they needed. After a six-day stand-off, we finally left the Seaman Guard Ohio.

Q Branch officers continued with their charade, but we weren't fooled by their talk of hospitals and medical checks, or them insisting we were only leaving the Seaman Guard Ohio temporarily. Sure enough, when we left the boat we weren't driven to any hospital. Instead, they took us to a police station, and that was it. I was going to prison.

We weren't stupid. We knew the building was Tuticorin police station, but still they kept up with their lies – or, at least, they avoided telling us the truth. Outside the police station it was chaos. Once again, the press seemed to have been tipped off to our arrival, and there was a mad scrum outside the building. The Estonians in our group didn't do any of us any favours. When they were escorted in, they decided to cover their faces for the cameras. This just made them look guilty, as if they had something to hide. Images of this scene were beamed around the world, and the way we looked at that point mattered. This would help to shape people's perceptions of us from the start. In the footage, you can see the bus arriving, and you can just make me out behind the bars of the cage. But there was no way I was covering my face that day. I had nothing to be ashamed about because I had done nothing wrong.

They kept us in the police station all day without food, water or any kind of comforts. Then officers asked us to sign something that was written in Tamil. We had no interpreter in the room to tell us what the document meant, or any legal representation to advise us, yet they expected us to sign something we couldn't read and didn't understand. No chance. They were having a laugh. We could have been signing a confession to anything for all we knew. We told them where to go.

We found out later that AdvanFort had sent a rep down to help us but, as soon as he saw what was happening, he fucked off sharpish because he was frightened that he might get arrested too, probably with good reason. The British Consulate apparently tried to get in to see us as well, but our officials were refused entry. The police never told us we were under arrest, or what charges might eventually be brought against us. We weren't allowed to see anyone, let alone a lawyer. As well as being corrupt, the legal system over there was an absolute joke. We were denied our rights from the start.

The language barrier didn't help. Officers couldn't even write out our names properly, even though all they had to do was copy them from our passports. In the UK, cases would be thrown out if police made mistakes in the documentation, but that never seemed to matter in India. The police did what they pleased. No-one tackled them on their conduct or practices, not the judge or the press.

They kept us there all day. Thirty-five men were crammed into a room together with no food and hardly any water. No-one could tell us what was going on, or they just couldn't be bothered to explain. To them, we probably didn't matter at all.

Looking back, it seems ironic that we were fully prepared in case a ship was attacked by armed and vicious Somali pirates, and we didn't imagine that the biggest threat to our wellbeing was going to come from the Indian coastguard, and their corrupt police and judicial system.

Later, we were told that if our names were on a charge sheet that was pretty much it: we were guilty in the eyes of the authorities, and the only way out was to pay someone. Curiously, the company agent received immunity, so how did that happen? Draw your own conclusions. We certainly did. Even the names of the company owners in America were on the charge sheet, but not the agent, even though he was representing the company and was present in the port. At one point, we saw him talking, laughing and joking with the police. From our perspective, it looked like a total stitch-up.

CHAPTER 14

PRISONER 6158

When we finally left the police station under escort it was growing dark. We were told we were being taken to the local court, but when we arrived it was closed. Our police escort took us round the back of the building and herded us onto the bus again. We drove for some time before the driver pulled over, stopped the engine, and we were all ordered off.

By the side of the road, the police commander started shouting at us. He was waving blank pieces of paper, calling out for us to sign them. He said, if we complied, we would be allowed to go back to our ship in a couple of days. He must have thought we were bloody idiots if he imagined we were going to believe that fairy story. They had already lied to us to get us off the boat, so we didn't trust them at all. Why would we sign a blank piece of paper? Anything could have been written above our signatures, up to and including a confession to a bunch of murders we knew nothing about. Everyone refused to sign. The police clearly weren't happy. The situation had the potential to become really nasty, but we still refused to sign their stupid bits of paper. The trouble was, it seemed like we were going nowhere until the issue had been resolved. In the end, I came up with a simple solution.

"Just sign the thing," I told the other lads, who must have thought I'd gone daft. "Write anything, put a squiggle, just don't sign your real name. This lot are too stupid to know the difference."

I put a squiggle on my piece of paper before handing it over. They seemed happy. I could have signed it Mickey Mouse, and they wouldn't have realised. The others all did the same and that was that. Moments later, we were back on the bus and on our way again.

The first prison we experienced was Palayamkottai Central Prison in Tirunelveli on the southern tip of India. The place dates back to the 1880s, and it certainly showed its age. The conditions there were so terrible I firmly believe that, if we had been made to serve our sentence there, some of our number would have died. That might sound dramatic, but I have no doubts about it.

To begin with, the place was completely over-crowded. It had an official capacity of 1,300, but there were around 3,000 prisoners when we arrived. The Indians were crammed in, with as many as 30 people or more packed into a single cell, which was crazy.

They stuck all of us into one very big room and made us sleep with the light on, which was almost impossible. Unsurprisingly, with the tension and the conditions, everyone ended up snapping at each other. One of the Indian guys, in particular, drove everybody crazy. He insisted on having his makeshift bath really early in the morning in that room. The place was like a big outhouse, and it looked like a toilet block. If we wanted a proper bath or shower, we were out of luck. Instead, we had to chuck a bucket of water over our heads. This Indian guy used to go through this noisy routine at four or five o'clock in the morning, waking everyone up. It didn't matter how much abuse we hurled at him, he wouldn't be told and, frankly, I am surprised he got out of there alive. He was lucky that we were actually law-abiding lads and not the evil men the authorities claimed we were. Real criminals would have murdered the dozy bastard.

Thankfully, we only spent three days and two nights in Palayamkottai before most of us were on the move again. The 12 Indians who were part our crew were kept there, and we were separated from them at this point. The authorities didn't seem to care about the Indians, but their reason for moving us was no act of kindness. They just needed us to stay alive and be healthy. If one us died in their prison, they would lose face in the eyes of the rest of the world.

I used to say to the lads, "If one of us drops down dead, be sure to have your bag packed because we'd be out of here. They won't be able to cover it up for long, and it won't end well for them." I was serious, but I had no idea how close I was to hitting on a truth, as time would eventually tell.

We were told that we were off to a different prison but, as it turned out, they weren't keeping all of us together. We went minus Paul Towers, who was kept back for further questioning. Unfortunately for Paul, the police were stuck on the idea that he was one of the main men on the ship, someone responsible for the wrongdoing that they were convinced had taken place. Paul had the misfortune to be in charge of the guns and ammo, and that was enough for him to be singled out as a ringleader.

The chief engineer, chief officer, second officer and the captain, Dudnik Valentyn, were also given the same treatment, and they were all taken for interrogation elsewhere. Paul told us about the experience later. It was dire by all accounts, and the barrage of questions was constant. The police were full of themselves, acting as if they had caught some big-time drugs mastermind or notorious gangster, not some ordinary bloke involved in a routine anti-piracy operation. He told us they were all high-fiving each other in celebration, like they had just landed some very big players. They were deluded. He kept spelling out the reality of our operation to the officers, but they weren't interested. In fact, his insistence on contradicting their story narked them even more. They kept telling him, "You are a very bad man and you will be punished," while trying to get him to confess to whatever the hell it was they thought he had done. Paul rarely ate – he was given little food anyway – and he didn't know what they were talking about, or why they thought he was such a high-profile catch. He didn't even know where he was. These guys treated him like a terrorist, not a bloke unlucky enough to be in the wrong place at the wrong time.

While Paul was under interrogation, we all piled onto a bus and were driven off to Puzhal Central Prison 2 in Chennai, 390 miles to the north on the east coast of India. We arrived late at night so we couldn't see much of the place, and we weren't able to form an opinion until daylight. Convicted criminals went next door, into the main jail, Central Prison 1, but this was the place where we were held on their equivalent of remand while we waited to see if we would be released, get bail, or be given a trial date.

At least this was a better prison than Palayamkottai Central. The cells were small but large enough to accommodate three or four of us. I was in with Billy and Roman. Paul Towers joined us once his wholly unnecessary interrogation was over. He was very hungry, and he looked absolutely exhausted.

We weren't the only foreigners this time. As well as us, there were Iranians, Sri Lankans and Nigerians banged up in there. Most of them were inside on drugs charges. The Iranians had a meth lab on the go before they were caught, but we got on all right with them considering our different natures and nationalities. We didn't have a lot of choice but to try to rub along with our fellow inmates – but we kept them at arm's length as much as possible.

The conditions in the prison were disgusting. We had to walk by a huge storm drain on our way to the kitchen, and it was putrid. The Indians thought nothing of pissing or even shitting in it. They lived like savages. All that human waste, combined with the extreme heat, meant the stench was horrendous.

Our fellow prisoners were not pleased to see us, and not just because we were white westerners. Word had reached the prison that we were "very bad men", and the tension rose as the days passed. The local press certainly didn't help. From the start, the Tamil media portrayed us as mercenaries, gun runners and even terrorists, which was ridiculous. According to the papers, we were very dangerous suspects who had been arrested before we were able to commit some unnamed atrocity. This had an obvious effect on our fellow inmates and a big impact on our safety. In the early days we were pelted with stones, and we had to move around the prison in groups for protection.

These weren't idle threats either. They wanted to kill us. We realised they meant business when Nick Simpson got twatted in the back of the head with a rock and was lucky to avoid serious injury. We kicked off about it with the guards. After that, we were given an escort when we went around the prison, but that was as good as useless because the guards didn't give a shit about any obligation towards our safety. They used to piss about or stand so far away from us as to make no difference. If anyone threw anything at us, they didn't try to catch the culprit, and most of the time they ignored any threat or incident.

The amount of abuse the local inmates threw our way left us in no doubt about their intentions. We all understood how much danger we were in. Although apprehensive, I wasn't scared. The prison inmates had no idea who they were dealing with. If we did end up in a brawl, with no guards present, they would be facing military-trained veterans. We'd have battered some skulls, assumed dominance, then told them to back off and stay away. Abuse, screaming and shouting didn't matter to me.

There may have been over 1,000 prisoners, but we were easily picked out as targets because we were the only white people in the jail. There were no other westerners there, and I concluded that was because no westerner, not even a desperate drug dealer, would want to spend their days in Tuticorin, which was a shit-hole, if they had the choice of the whole of India.

The prison was open from the moment we were let out of our cells at 6am until 6pm. With the guards never around, for 12 hours a day we were targets for anybody with a grudge, fuelled by the nonsense they read in the local paper. But soon the novelty of our presence wore off and tensions slowly eased. It helped that we were a big group of tough men who could all handle ourselves. But, if we were in any doubt how dangerous it could be in there and why we could never get complacent, we soon had a shocking eye opener.

Some inmate obviously had a serious beef with another Indian guy because we came across him with his throat slashed. I don't know how he survived the attack, but he did. We saw this poor bloke just sitting there, holding his hand hard against the open wound, blood pouring through his fingers. No-one helped him or raised the alarm. It was just part and parcel of daily life in Central Prison. It was that kind of place.

The superintendent, the equivalent of a British prison governor, was a decent enough guy. He was a tall man who wore a beige, prison officer's uniform and usually had a smile on his face, probably because he was happy that he had secured a pretty good job. Mostly he seemed bemused by our situation.

He must have wondered what the hell we were doing there. He understood how a prison worked, but he could see there was something different about us. We weren't like most of the inmates in his prison, and not just because of our colour. He sensed we didn't belong there. He spoke to us with respect and he was polite, but we knew his hands were tied and there was nothing he could do about our situation. Q Branch was running the show. On our first day, he gave us some Bidis, their little cigarettes, and he got us some dahl, but the rice looked dodgy, so we passed up his offer. Eventually, we managed to get hold of some boiled potatoes, some eggs and onion. We made an omelette, and we survived on that instead.

For most of the day, we were separated from the general population of the jail, which was just as well. We tried to keep ourselves to ourselves, but that wasn't always possible. When we went down to the cook house, which we had to do every morning, we ran the gauntlet every step of the way. The Indian prisoners used to become very agitated when they knew we were coming. They would shout abuse and chuck whatever they could lay their hands on.

The Indian prisoners probably had no idea what we were supposed to have done, and I doubt they cared all that much. We were westerners and that was enough to make us a target for their abuse and their missiles. This prison was big. It was nearly a mile to the cook house, which was a very long way to walk under a constant barrage of abuse and stones. That ordeal was made even worse on the days when we arrived at the cook house to find there was no food left, or what was available was rotten and inedible.

This wasn't like prisons in the UK where an inmate would queue, and trustees would give him a plateful of something to eat. We had to make all our food ourselves, scavenging whatever we could find around the cook house. We quickly organised into a routine, creating cooking teams, with everyone taking a turn. What did we make? Stew. It was stew every day or, as we called it, "Stew of the day". Basically, it was the same bloody stew every day. Even that wasn't easy to make. We weren't chefs and there wasn't much meat. We used to get potatoes, green beans, cabbage, tomatoes and, if we were lucky, chicken necks and legs.

We quickly learnt to head straight to the kitchen first thing in the morning to beat the rush. I wouldn't even pause to piss. Every day in that cook house was a battle. We were coming to blows just to get hold of a pan, and we would have to kick off to make sure we had enough food to survive. Everyone was out for themselves. We had to cook for more than 20 people, and it could take us hours to assemble enough food so everyone would have even a minimal amount to eat. What was supposed to be lunch was often dished up at teatime because it took so long to put together all the ingredients we needed. Then we still had to cook the stew before we could even think about eating. A meal could take 12 hours.

In the morning we at least got eggs to boil, which we would have with chapatis, the unleavened bread they eat in India. But even getting hold of water to heat presented problems. There wasn't a tap close to the cell, so we had to bring water back from the cook house. We had to carry it in a big, heavy pail, like the ones people used to carry milk. If we were lucky, we'd get a trolley but, if not, we had to carry the bloody thing for a mile just so we could have water in the morning. Looking back, I was glad I had experienced the stretcher race and the log race during P Company, although I had no idea it was preparing me to carry a huge water pail for over a mile in the heat so I could have an egg in the morning.

Over time, we managed to get together our own pots, so it wasn't such a mad free-for-all in the cook house every day. We complained to the consulate, and officials put pressure on the prison to make sure we didn't starve to death. Occasionally, one of the lads might have a moan about the consulate not doing enough for us, but I would say, "Where do you think you are, the

Hilton Hotel?" We were stuck in prison, and there wasn't much our officials could do except remind the authorities that the UK was watching how its citizens were being treated.

At that point, I wasn't thinking ahead or figuring out when we were likely to be released. I was trying to take each day as it came, and simply survive. It didn't help that I had little or no idea what was going on beyond the prison walls. What was AdvanFort doing to secure our release? I didn't know. How was my ordeal affecting my family? Aside from what I learned from the occasional letters from home, brought in by consular staff on their occasional visits, I could only guess. What was my family keeping from me? How worried were they? How much distress had I caused them? Dwelling on all that 24/7 would have driven me mad, so I tried to think like a Para. Adapt and overcome.

None of us knew exactly what to expect when we first arrived at Puzhal Central Prison 2. We had no idea how long we would be locked up before we went to a trial. At that stage, we didn't know for sure if there would be a trial at all. We were left facing a lengthy period locked up on remand until the Indian authorities, who had our fate in their hands, decided whether to put us before a trial judge to answer trumped-up charges. Either way, it didn't look good for us.

I gained an idea of how things really worked by talking with one of the less hostile Indian inmates. None of what he told me was reassuring. He said that people were locked up in Puzhal 2 for at least six months, even for minor stuff, like breaking the terms of their visa. I realised there was going to be no quick fix and that

I had to accept I could be in prison for up to half a year. I was gutted. It was a desperate situation but, at that point, I set my hopes on six months as the maximum amount of time I would have to endure this hell-hole. And maybe it would turn out better. After a few months in jail, they might just say, "Right, there's your slap on the wrist." And then they'd let us go home. I had to believe that. The alternatives didn't bear thinking about.

I was furious it had come to this, but there was nothing I could do, so I took one day at a time and waited to see what would happen.

With the thought of six months in mind, I had to develop a sure-fire strategy to get through the days and weeks. I needed to stand on my own two feet, and us lads needed to work together. I had to suck it up, buttercup. I told myself I could be upset in my own time, but, for now, I had to safeguard my mental strength. That meant never allowing myself to look weak or seem down in the dumps. That strategy was often put to the test, and especially so in the run-up to Christmas.

We were arrested in October, so Christmas meant this ordeal had been dragging on for nearly three months with no end in sight. Whenever our case came up for review, we were ordered to appear in court via video. Because they didn't want us to leave jail, we'd be taken into a compound where we could see the judge on the screen, sitting in the Tuticorin District Principal Sessions Court. We'd be asked to state our name and prison number. Mine was 6158. Like my British Army serial number, it's imprinted on my brain, and I will never forget it. Those four digits represented who I was in the eyes of the judge and our jailers. I was only ever a number to them.

India always gave the impression it was 100 years behind the rest of the world, so video-court felt like a rare encounter with the modern world. But any hopes we had that these appearances might lead to progress on our case quickly evaporated. The judge would say, "two weeks", and that was it. There was no more from him. We didn't even receive the benefit of an explanation. The first time we went through this process, we were left wondering what he even meant by "two weeks". It turned out this was his way of delaying our hearing yet again. Because he didn't give a damn about any of us, he couldn't even be bothered to explain he was sending us back to rot in prison for another fortnight.

The food was terrible and scarce, so we never had enough to eat, and I lost a lot of weight. When Lisa flew out to see me, for my 28th birthday on 1 March 2014, she was shocked by my appearance. The place was dirty, insanitary, and there were cockroaches and other foul insects everywhere. We spent months living like that, and all that time we had to cope with the ever-present threat of violence erupting at any moment. Being a Para helped me. We were supposed to be ready for anything – it was our regimental motto – but there was one twist I wasn't quite ready for and, when it happened, I wasn't the only one freaked out by it.

One night we were sitting in the cell, playing Battleships of all things. I looked up and saw a huge, brown rat. It had calmly marched into our cell and was just sniffing around, as if it was evaluating our accommodation. This wasn't like the rats you might see in the UK. Native British rodents were usually a bit larger than a mouse and maybe could stretch to the size of a small squirrel. This thing was enormous. It was the size of a bloody cat!

I stood up and yelled "Rat!", but before we had time to react it had turned and scuttled away.

That night, the lights were switched off and we were trying to get to sleep. My makeshift bed was in a corner near the toilet. Something woke me. I was groggy and couldn't quite work out what was going on. Then I felt something tickle my feet...

I looked up but couldn't see anything at first, so I lay back down and turned to face the wall. That was when I found myself with that massive rat only inches away. I leapt up and yelled. This huge thing shot over me then jumped towards one of the other guys. Because I was yelling, Billy sat bolt upright, and the rat bashed into him before fleeing.

We were all so freaked out by our visitor, we made sure our beds were reinforced from then on. We used mosquito nets, pieces of cardboard, and anything else we could find, all tied down with string. Thankfully, I never had another incident with one of those cat-sized rats, but I will never forget that massive bugger's furry face so close to mine!

CHAPTER 15

LISA'S STORY: PIRATES & TERRORISTS

When Nick told us he wanted to move into close protection, we agreed it seemed a logical move. Then he mentioned anti-piracy work. I remember thinking, pirates? Do they still have them in this day and age? I didn't have a clue. Nick explained who they were, where they were from, and what they were doing, and I understood the need to protect vessels on the sea. When you see pictures of these modern-day pirates and the weapons they carry, you realise what they actually are. They are terrorists.

Even so, I didn't think Nick was likely to end up in an actual battle with pirates, so I never really worried too much about that. My biggest concern was the sea. I knew it could get very rough, and I had seen footage of boats getting battered about by typhoons. Nick could swim, but I didn't think he was a very strong swimmer, so I was more concerned he might drown rather than anything else.

He did a few jobs on board ships and they seemed to go well. We thought it was all going to work out. Nick would ring when he was ashore, so he never felt too far away. He would tell us where he was going and when he was likely to get there, and he would call when he reached port.

He called me before he went aboard the Seaman Guard Ohio to tell me he would soon be on his way to Sri Lanka and he would call me again when he hit dry land. When he didn't call as promised, I asked around to find out if anyone else had heard from him. No-one had, but they all assured me he'd be fine. Dad said that maybe Nick had jumped on a different transit. We heard about the typhoon in the area and thought his vessel might have had been delayed.

The following afternoon, I was getting ready to pop out when mam phoned me. She said, "Don't panic, Lisa…" As soon as she said that, I knew what she was calling about. She said Nick had phoned and he was fine, but there was something happening with the boat, and he was stuck in India. My mam didn't fully understand what was going on because the picture was confusing, but Nick had promised he would call back. When he phoned me direct, he sounded calm. He told me, "These idiots are making an absolute shit-show of this. They have brought the ship into port and they are making a right meal of it, but everything will be fine, and we will be on our way again soon."

He told me the name of the company. I did some digging and found out AdvanFort was based in America. I promised I'd give the company a ring and find out what was happening. I called AdvanFort and the person on the phone explained they had an Indian agent out there. He was going to visit the vessel soon, and then he would ring me with an update.

When the agent called, he said there was nothing to worry about, it was all just procedure. Nick called us a few times while he was stuck on the boat. He was bored but not too worried.

When the agent called again, he told me it was all sorted, and the lads would be on their way in the morning. There was no concern in his voice or Nick's when he phoned again, so I assumed it would be resolved the next day.

The following night, I was sleeping, so I missed a call from Nick that came at 3.40am. He phoned mam instead and told her what was happening. He called me back and, this time, I was fully awake. Nick said, "It's not getting sorted today." He told me, "We are being arrested, and I don't know what's happening or when I'll get to speak to you again."

Despite the shock, I immediately started thinking about the practicalities. "Where is your passport?" I asked him, because I didn't want him to leave it behind on the boat. He said the police had taken it from him already. All he had was a picture of it on his phone. I knew we couldn't just let him get arrested without doing something to help, so I promised I would phone our MP as soon as his office opened later that morning.

He said, "Lisa I have to go." And that was that.

It was such a shock to be called in the middle of the night. I sat up in bed, staring at the phone, wondering if it was all a bad dream. There was no way I could get back to sleep, and it was a restless night as I tried to figure out what would happen next. I spoke to my parents early that morning. We still believed everything would be sorted. I never doubted Nick's innocence. Dad asked him if anything illegal was going on, but he never believed for a moment Nick had committed a crime. He just thought Nick might have become accidentally involved in something dodgy – maybe there was illicit cargo on board that he didn't know about, something like that. But there was nothing. We simply couldn't understand why the authorities had arrested the men.

I contacted our MP in Ashington, Ian Lavery, and I spoke to Grace, his secretary. I told her I was giving Ian a heads-up to see if there was anything he could do, even though we didn't know how serious the situation was. I told Grace the men had all been arrested, and we needed help from the Foreign Office. Ian really helped. He was a good source of support, and he was always asking if there was anything more he could do. He never once turned his back on Nick, or any of the lads. He was always the one in parliamentary meetings who stood up and raised their case. He made sure he called them "six military veterans from the UK" so he wasn't just fighting for his sole constituent. This helped to keep the men's plight in the public eye. Later, as the weeks and months went by, it became apparent this was an issue that had grown too big for just one MP to take on. Fortunately, Ian had been in contact with the Foreign Office from the start, and their officials had become involved.

We didn't hear back from the Foreign Office straight away, and that weekend was the longest of my life. It dragged on and on. We were naïve. We assumed all of this could be sorted easily if only the Foreign Office would just step in and tell the Indian authorities the men had done nothing wrong. The crew had all the right documents, and everything was in order, so the authorities should just let them go.

That was my hope. In reality, I didn't hear back from the Foreign Office for a few days. By that stage, Nick was already in a second prison.

I was sitting in the back office with two of my line managers when I received a call from the Foreign Office. The caller said they had a message from Nick. He was absolutely fine. He wanted me not to worry about him and it would all be over soon. So, don't panic. The Foreign Office gave us no indication how long this ordeal was likely to last.

We also had a visit from a guy called Malcolm from AdvanFort. He was a team leader, and he visited the six families to bring us up to speed. He came to my house and explained that the men on the boat had done nothing wrong, and that this was just an admin error. He initially thought they'd be held for the weekend then they'd be free. I got the impression this was the most likely outcome, and I consoled myself thinking this detour might even prove a bit of an adventure for Nick. Not a nice one for sure but, eventually, it would end up as a family anecdote, about that time Nick was banged up in India for a couple of days.

It took us a while before the horrible reality began to sink in, and we realised this was not a simple matter that was going to be sorted quickly. Time passed. Days grew into weeks, and the weeks eventually became months, and nothing was being done to get the men out of prison. I felt so helpless and frustrated. I just kept thinking, why is my brother in India? I just didn't understand. Nobody could tell us the reason because nobody knew.

In those early days, there was no way I considered that this might go on to last for four long years. After each court hearing, we tried to tease out more information. We were never off Google. I was trying to find similar cases and tracking down anyone who might be able to help. Most of the time, we were left with more questions than answers. Was this action by the Indians a result of the terrorist attacks across Mumbai in 2008? As crazy as it sounded, the press in India were linking our Nick to Al Qaeda. Here was a white, western, British ex-paratrooper being discussed as if he were connected to an Islamic terrorist organisation. This idea was gaining serious traction in the articles we found online. It was crazy. Mam even found a YouTube video of the arrest, and we could see Nick in the footage. Underneath the caption read, "Sailor or Spy?" He wasn't either of those things. Someone was spreading dangerous lies.

These ridiculous reports would have been a joke if it wasn't for the fact that people were taking these lies seriously with the result that no-one was able to get Nick out of prison. We certainly weren't laughing. We were just desperate to bring my brother home.

CHAPTER 16

WHY WE ARE REALLY HERE

So much of what happens to us in life comes down to luck. We all have free will, and we are in charge of the direction we take, but the decisions we make, even the ones that seem insignificant, can have such a huge impact on our lives, though we don't always know it at the time.

When I thought about my life, as I did every day in prison, it kept coming back to turning points: the different directions I could have taken that would have kept me from Chennai and out of jail. What if I had stayed in the Paras? What if I'd left sooner? Or a year later? What if I had enough money to take up a close protection course immediately after I had left the regiment and decided against maritime work? I could have signed on for a rotation working for a different company, or ended up on another job, which would have seen me board then leave the Seaman Guard Ohio at a different time. All the decisions I took, big and small, put me exactly in the wrong place at exactly the wrong time.

Because none of us knew why we were in jail, everyone was full of questions all the time. We started to wonder if our arrest was linked somehow to another issue we knew nothing about. We had so much time on our hands, we started to overthink everything, and we could have easily missed a truth simply because we weren't seeing anything clearly any more. We didn't know what was going on, so we started to make up our own conspiracy theories. We couldn't help it. Was this the company's fault in some way? Had AdvanFort been doing something illegal that was much bigger than our brief presence in Indian waters with a few barrels of dodgy diesel? That was a worry, because we would then be the ones to take the rap for something serious that we were unaware of.

We found out later that the company was in the clear. AdvanFort was as innocent as we were. The only wrong in the entire saga was the method the fishermen used to deliver the fuel to the Seaman Guard Ohio – and that was hardly a serious transgression in a place like India.

Throughout my time trapped in that country, I asked myself the same question over and over: why? Why are they doing this to us? What possible reason could the Indian authorities have for arresting and jailing so many men when they must have known we had done absolutely nothing wrong? It made no sense at all to any of us. But then we began to hear stories about an unrelated incident and suddenly some light was shed on our predicament.

This incident, 18 months before, had caused massive international and diplomatic ructions. I was only partially aware of the circumstances, and we weren't involved in any way, but it was possible that what happened in the Enrica Lexie case was having a huge effect on our lives.

On 15 February 2012, off the coast of Kerala, Italian Marines on board an oil tanker called the Enrica Lexie allegedly opened fire on Indian fishermen who they had mistakenly identified as pirates. Two men, named Ajesh Binki and Valentine, were shot dead on their fishing boat, the St Antony. The killings caused a major row and a massive rift between Italy and India – which still rumbles on to this day. The ship was intercepted by the Indian Navy, and the two Italian Marines – Massimiliano Latorre and Salvatore Girone – were charged with murder.

On the face of it, I couldn't understand why those Marines had opened fire on the fishing boats in the first place. There was an established routine which armed security guards had to follow before they resorted to lethal force. The aim of these protocols was to avoid pointless deaths, like those of Ajesh Binki and Valentine.

There were loads of vessels off the coast of India. We weren't allowed simply to open fire on every skiff or fishing boat even if it had happened to sail too close for comfort and ignored warnings. Sometimes it was hard to determine intent, or distinguish one vessel from the next, but we had to do our job as highly-trained professionals.

I don't care what anyone else says about it, in my opinion, those Italian Marines effectively murdered two innocent fishermen. There was no way you can gloss over that. Something went very wrong – and it shouldn't have done. The Italian Marines failed to follow their protocols properly. Indian fishing vessels would approach all the time because they were curious. They would see big ships and would want to take a look. That was all.

Of course, this being India, any sympathy I might have had for the authorities following this awful tragedy was eroded by the actions of the judicial system. The authorities detained the men without charge for two and four years respectively while the diplomatic row blew up around them. India was criticised by the European Parliament for a serious breach in human rights in holding the Marines without charge, and relationships between India and the EU became seriously strained. The row also saw questions raised at the UN and NATO, and the increased pressure and profile of the case led to the release of the two suspects. This outcome left the Indian authorities angry, resentful, and itching to take it out on someone else as soon as they had the chance. And then we showed up in the Seaman Guard Ohio.

The authorities couldn't wait to get hold of another band of "foreign mercenaries", as they viewed us. We had the extreme misfortune to be the next people in their sights, and we were going to pay for the sins of the Italians, as they saw it. If you think our link with the Enrica Lexie affair is just another one of our conspiracy theories, then think again. It was the main reason we were arrested and imprisoned. How do we know this? Because the authorities made little secret of the fact. We were repeatedly told in the clearest of terms, "That is why you are here."

We were made an example of, because the Indian authorities had effectively let the Italians slip through their fingers. They didn't care if we were innocent or guilty, they just wanted us to go down. Everything else was a smokescreen to disguise and justify what they were doing to us. We were pawns to them, and we were plunged into this horrible nightmare just so they could make a point to the rest of the world. It didn't matter that we weren't Italian and had nothing to do with the Enrica Lexie case. We were foreign, and we were next. The Indians were so resentful of the Italian Marines that they created a massive fiction out of our situation then sold it to the world. We would be a warning to others.

The Italians were lucky. Their actions were classed as an international case because the shootings happened at sea. They also had the advantage of being active Marines in the Italian armed forces. This helped to make this a higher grade diplomatic incident between two countries than ours turned out to be. The British government had some responsibility for us as UK subjects, of course, but there wasn't the same level of involvement that would have followed if we had been serving soldiers.

In the end, there was insufficient evidence to charge the Italians and they eventually walked. They didn't do any jail time, not even on remand. As the diplomatic row rumbled on, they sat in the Italian embassy for years before they were eventually allowed to leave the country and go home. Things were different for us because we were arrested in Tamil Nadu. We came to understand that the authorities could do whatever they liked with us, and it was likely that no-one would intervene.

Even though I now understood the real reason for our arrest, it didn't stop me from questioning my own responsibility, wondering if things could have worked out far better for me if only I had acted differently. The police had told us plainly we were being held because of the actions of those Italian Marines, but the same questions ran round and round my brain. Why us and, in particular, why me? It wasn't just that I was feeling sorry for myself. It was the crazy long odds that had led me here. Of all the people the Indian authorities could have chosen to arrest in order to make their twisted point to the rest of the world, why did they have to choose my ship and our crew? Was it just plain bad luck or did we, on some strange cosmic level I didn't understand, somehow deserve this? If we did, I struggled to see how.

I felt no regret or shame for anything I had done while on operations as a Para in either Iraq or Afghanistan. I always handled myself like a professional soldier, and I had never done anything that contravened the rules of war or the Geneva Convention. This was not a case of the universe taking revenge on a soldier who had turned rogue. I'd done everything by the book. And yet I was still here, trapped in Chennai.

Maybe all my luck exploded in a puff of smoke when I was blown up in Afghanistan and I managed to walk away from that wrecked Land Rover with barely a scratch. How many of my nine lives had I used up when we missed that far bigger – and likely fatal – land mine by just a few feet? These questions dogged me day and night.

CHAPTER 17

BRIBING OUR WAY OUT

People are understandably curious to know what role AdvanFort played during my captivity. They assume that our employer moved heaven and earth to get us out of prison and, at the very least, did its best to look after us while we were over there.

Most people also incorrectly assume that I carried on getting paid all the while I was out in India. That would have been the right and decent thing for AdvanFort to do. Some of the men had wives and families with bills and mortgages to pay, and we were only in jail because we happened to be aboard one of the company's ships. If I hadn't been working for AdvanFort, I'd have still been a free man. But the truth was AdvanFort abandoned us and quickly stopped paying us. I lost thousands of pounds in wages which I should have earned during the four years I was trapped helpless in India.

The last direct contact we had with the company was while I was still on the ship and Paul Towers messaged the company reps in the UK to tell them we were getting arrested.

We only found out much later that AdvanFort sent a Polish guy who worked for the company to the police station to see if he could do anything but, once he worked out what was going on, he panicked and scarpered pretty sharpish, it seems. I suppose he was worried he might suffer the same fate as us. He was probably right about that, but he certainly didn't do anything to improve our situation before he left. The Indian authorities also wanted to arrest Samir Farajallah, the billionaire company owner, who was based in the US, as well as any other company officials they could get their hands on, but that plan never worked out.

In the end, we received almost nothing from AdvanFort. The company arranged a lawyer for us and paid for our legal services at first, but that eventually stopped. In the end, we had to find the money for lawyers ourselves. I got the impression AdvanFort was far more concerned about reclaiming its ship than helping the men who were risking their lives to make the company a profit.

At the outset, we were all very angry. We began to suspect the company had done something seriously wrong, and we were the fall guys. But that turned out not to be the case. We discovered AdvanFort did nothing that was against the law.

While we were on remand, we knew that there had to be all sorts going on behind the scenes, and we were pretty sure a lot of it would be dodgy. I had already gained a sense of the level of corruption in India. There were constant rumours of money changing hands to speed things along, or to get someone released who wouldn't otherwise be freed.

Months later, we were told by someone who worked for the company that AdvanFort was approached in those early days by the police. According to what we were told, officers asked the company to hand over a substantial bribe to get us out and the Seaman Guard

Ohio released. There was talk of a meeting between the police and a representative of the company during which the subject of a pay-off arose. According to what we were told, this would have made the whole problem conveniently disappear.

Although we could never confirm the story, we were told that the police demanded several "crore" in return for dropping the case. A crore is ten million Indian rupees, which was the equivalent of around £120,000. Allegedly, this lot of chancers asked for a bribe of seven crore – or £784,000 – to free us and our vessel. Imagine if a police officer in the UK was discovered to have asked for a bribe of over three-quarters of a million pounds. He would be jailed for years in disgrace. But, over there, this kind of wheeler-dealing was so widespread it was an accepted part of the system. The corruption had to reach everywhere, we supposed, because whoever was asking for the money would have to split the pot with all his colleagues and anyone who had a direct influence on, or connection to, the case. This would have to have been an expensive and extensive scam involving a lot of people at all levels.

We were told there was some argument in that meeting about the amount the police were demanding, and this turned into a haggle. The offer by police was allegedly amended. Give us five crore, instead of seven, and we'll drop the charges. That was the rumoured deal. According to what we were told, company officials were being asked to pay a bribe of half a million quid to get the ship and the men back, but it seemed there was no way that AdvanFort was going to agree to that.

All that was speculation, of course, but it certainly wouldn't have surprised me if that was how it did play out. What I witnessed in India demonstrated just how systematically corrupt everything was. The police, in particular, were greedy, money-oriented people, looking to cash in whenever they could. Though I wasn't in the room, AdvanFort made it clear to the families of the imprisoned men that things were worked out with money changing hands. Bribes had been demanded but refused, we were told.

The last thing I wanted to see was bent police officers getting wealthy out of blackmailing the company, but it seemed that was the only way to get real justice in Chennai. AdvanFort had just secured a large contract with Cypriot shipping owners, so executives could have easily paid a ransom if a deal was on offer, but it seems no payment was made. They probably never thought we were worth it, to be honest.

We will never know for sure exactly what went on in those meetings, but we stayed in jail, and nothing more was ever said about it. Maybe company executives had questioned why they should have to pay a bribe when neither they, nor their employees, had done anything seriously wrong. We just didn't know. Some of the lads wondered why AdvanFort didn't go public and expose police for soliciting bribes but, in all honesty, what good would that have done us? We would have still been in jail, and the police would have simply lied through their teeth to deny that any such thing ever happened. Worse still, there would have been a backlash against us. Someone would likely whisper in the judge's ear, and suddenly our sentences would be much longer.

The nerve of those corrupt police officers was staggering, and it still makes me angry when I think about their actions. In my eyes, extorting money made them as bad as the Somali pirates who raided the ships we were hired to protect. The police were worse, in fact, because the pirates never pretended to be honourable men with a public duty to uphold the rule of law. I had more respect for the actual pirates than this bunch of extortioners. At least you knew where you stood with the pirates. They dealt with you straight. There was no justice in a country when justice could be bought – and justice remained our only hope.

CHAPTER 18

LISA'S STORY: GUARDIAN ANGEL

The constant stress about Nick took a toll on all of us, but particularly my mam. She already had a lot on her plate because she looked after my Auntie Joan, who had Down's Syndrome and Alzheimer's and needed a lot of help.

Mam started to get headaches which became worse and worse. Finally, they became so unbearable she went to the doctor to get herself checked out. He thought the same as the rest of us: that mam had a lot going on, and the stress of it all was making her ill. Headaches just seemed like a typical reaction to the circumstances, so we didn't think it was anything more than that. We had no idea how poorly she actually was.

On 21 December, a little over two months after Nick was arrested, she went to have her hair done. She wasn't planning on going, but I persuaded her, thinking it would make her feel better. That day, I had just sent my parents a message informing them that a chaplain from the Mission To Seafarer's was going to try to visit Nick, which was good news because the authorities had not allowed him inside the prison before. I told my parents, if they had a message to give him, they should send it to me as soon as possible so I could pass it on.

Not long after, my phone rang. My mam's number appeared on the screen. I became flustered because I couldn't really speak in the office. I answered and snapped, "Mam, I'm at work!" But it wasn't her, it was the hairdresser. She said something was wrong with mam. Something had happened and she wasn't speaking. She had collapsed in the chair and wasn't really with it. The hairdresser said she had been fine up till that moment. She had been busy showing everyone the petition we'd started calling for Nick's release. That was normal for mam because she used to carry the petition round with her everywhere, trying to get strangers to sign. Next thing, she had just collapsed, and people had called an ambulance.

I wasn't overly worried about her at that point. I just thought she had passed out because of the stress. I assumed she would be all right. I told my colleagues that I needed to go. I said I didn't know what had happened, but my mam was being taken to Wansbeck General Hospital in Ashington.

Craig, my line manager, insisted on coming with me, which was very kind of him. He later told me that he had guessed how serious the situation was before I twigged. We reached the hospital before my mam, and I could only watch as she was carried in from the ambulance, lying unconscious on a stretcher. I was shouting, "Mam!" as if I expected her to wake up. I was in a daze. A paramedic managed to get me inside to a place where I could sit and wait. We were sat there forever, it seemed. When the doctor finally came to see us, he asked if there was anyone with me because he didn't want to speak to me on my own. He could see I was in shock, and what he said was likely to go in one ear and out the other. He was asking questions about her medication, and then he said, "We think it's a bleed." It didn't sink in. I still thought she would just wake up and she would be fine.

Craig rang my Auntie Carol who he already knew because they had worked together. I alerted dad. He collected my brother Paul and brought him to the hospital. We were all there with my mam now, but she was still unconscious. She didn't wake up for days.

We knew we were likely to be waiting for some time. That meant we needed to sort out some practicalities. Mam had a little puppy, called Cassie, who was only a year old. One of us would have to go to the house to look after her. Her bag containing her house keys was still at the hairdressers'. By the time me and dad arrived there, the shop was shut. I had a spare key, but it turned out it wouldn't work because it hadn't been cut properly. I was stuck outside mam's house in a complete state, trying to get inside so I could see to the dog and wondering if I should phone work to see if anyone there could help me break in. Then the phone rang. The hairdresser was calling to see how mam was. I was just manic by then. I said, "I need to get into your shop." She opened up to let me get mam's bag and the keys, and we went back to mam's house and retrieved the dog.

While I was away, mam was rushed to Royal Victoria Infirmary in Newcastle, under blue lights. Paul and Auntie Carol had followed the ambulance and they were told they had an important decision to make. They had to decide whether or not the medical team should go ahead and operate. Mam had suffered an aneurysm, a rupture of a weakened artery in the brain. Paul and Carol were told she would die if the surgeons didn't operate and, even if they did, she would have serious, lifelong issues to deal with. The medical staff explained that some people might not want to have the surgery and carry on living afterwards. Since my mam was unconscious, she couldn't consent to the operation, so our Paul and Carol had to give permission. Paul said, "She is only 59 years old. Please do whatever you can." We thank God every single day that he made the right decision.

We waited a long time to find out how the operation went. All those hours of uncertainty were awful. When Malcom from AdvanFort heard about my mam, he turned up at the RVI and sat with us for hours. I think the poor man felt a lot of guilt because he had been the one who employed the men and put them on that vessel. Now the pressure of that situation had *put my mam's life at risk. The doctors explained to us that she would have inevitably suffered the aneurysms anyway, so Nick's imprisonment definitely wasn't the cause. But the stress was a contributing factor.*

When the operation was finally over, I went with my Auntie Carol to see my mam. Her head was bandaged, there were tubes coming out of her mouth and nose, and she looked terrible. Seeing her like that, I had my first-ever panic attack. I didn't think they existed until then, but now, because of all that's happened, I am very familiar with anxiety. I thought I was going to pass out. I remember trying to claw at my jumper because suddenly I felt incredibly hot. The hospital staff had to put a fan on me and pour water down my throat to cool me down. My Auntie Carol was crying, and I was in such a bad way I was screaming.

Mam was in intensive care for seven days then in the high dependency ward for a couple of weeks. For all that time we didn't know if she would live or die. Only when she left the high dependency ward did we start to think that maybe she was going to pull through. Even then the doctors kept saying that her recovery would be a very long process. She was in hospital for four months, and she had irreversible, life-long damage.

The next day the consultant and surgeon came to see us. My mam's surgeon, Nick Ross, was phenomenal. He saved her life with that operation. He said, "Your mam has got a guardian angel watching over her. We didn't think she would make it through the night, but she did."

Our thoughts turned to Nick straightaway, and how we could let him know what had happened. Dad was growing more and more angry. He was saying the British government would have to get him home now, and surely the Indian authorities would release him once they had found out what had happened to his mother.

We didn't want Nick to hear by chance about mam, or to find out only a few sketchy details, because we knew he would worry and feel even more helpless than we did. The Consular girls had already done their Christmas visit and weren't due to return to the prison for a few weeks. But Sharon agreed to go back. I was determined that Nick would get a message directly from us, so I asked her to read him out exactly what I had written about mam's health. She then handed him another letter that contained more information.

It was almost the new year, around 10 days after mam first collapsed, before we could tell Nick what had happened. That was deliberate. I wanted to wait so we could tell him she was stable. I did not want him to worry that she was going to die, not while he was stuck thousands of miles away in prison and helpless. I don't know if it was the right decision or the wrong one but that was why we made it.

It was so good of Sharon to go in and see Nick to give him the news. It must have been difficult for her. At the operational level, I always found that the Foreign Office and consulate people acted with professionalism. We were beginning to have serious reservations about those at the top, the decision makers who never did enough to get Nick and the other men released. I found myself wanting to hate them all, but I was always very grateful to the Foreign Office and embassy staff who helped get family letters into Nick while he was a prisoner in Chennai.

Mam has continued to make a long and extremely slow recovery. It is much slower than we hoped or anticipated but, really, she is a medical miracle. She has no speech, although she can say the odd word. She understands what you are saying to her as long as you talk slowly and keep the conversation basic. Mam's brain can't keep up when we talk too fast. She walks with aids or uses a wheelchair for longer journeys, but she manages to live on her own in an adapted property, with carers coming in. I see her every single day to make sure that she is OK. When I look back now, it still frightens me to think how close we came to losing her.

I'll always believe that the reason mam is still with us today is because she wasn't going anywhere until she knew her youngest was back home safe.

CHAPTER 19

THE WORST NEWS

I had been banged up in prison for two months when I received the worst possible news from home. Sharon from the consulate told me that my mam was seriously, dangerously ill. While I was stuck in Chennai, completely helpless and unable to do anything, my brother and sister were at my mam's bedside. I was told mam had been rushed to hospital. She'd had a double aneurysm, and it was incredibly serious. So bad, in fact, she hadn't been expected to live.

I knew an aneurysm was a massive and rapid injury to the brain which could cause huge internal bleeding. One aneurysm was very serious, and the chances of survival were around one-in-two. Mam had a double aneurysm. People don't often recover from that. One doctor said the survival rate was less than one per cent.

I was stuck in India while my family had been given a very stark choice. The hospital needed their consent to operate. If they agreed to surgery, it might save my mam's life, but there was also a chance that she could die. They were then told that if they did not give permission for the operation, she would definitely die. It was a huge responsibility but, really, it was no choice at all. They had no option but to consent to the surgery that would, at least, give mam some hope of survival.

I was thousands of miles away. I couldn't do anything to help the rest of my family, let alone my mam. All they could do was put her in the hands of the surgeons and hope for the best. It was a long operation and a very risky one, but those guys did a fantastic job. The surgeons saved my mam's life and, somehow, she made it through.

I was grateful that the consulate took the trouble to keep me updated about my mam. Officials made sure they saw us twice a month, which was very good of them. Normally, they saw imprisoned British nationals once every three months, but I think they visited us more frequently because they realised we were different. They could see we had done nothing wrong, and they knew the impact that this injustice was likely to have on us, mentally and physically, a welfare concern that was highlighted by the campaigners back home. Whatever high-level decisions the Foreign Office made in India and London regarding us, we couldn't fault the people on the ground. They tried their best to help us through this ordeal. The girls from the consulate were really helpful, passing letters to and from our families. This was vitally important because we couldn't trust the jail to handle mail properly. I once wrote a letter that ended up stuck in the jailer's desk for two weeks before he could be bothered to put it in the post.

There came a point when everyone had to accept that we were going to be stuck in prison over Christmas and the New Year. We knew it would be hard, but we would just have to deal with it. In the end, there was no way we could celebrate the day at all. We couldn't do anything special, like cook a Christmas meal, because we didn't have the ingredients. The day was just like any other that we spent banged up in Chennai. The consulate paid us a visit and brought us cake and a few gifts, which was very good of them, but we couldn't do anything else except try not to think too much about our families back home, and how much we were missing them. We knew, in turn, they would be sitting there, feeling as if there was a big hole in the family Christmas, with their loved ones all stuck out here.

My sister had been planning to come out to visit me, but then my mam was taken ill. Lisa wrote to me explaining why she wasn't able to come. I fully understood, of course. She had to be there in Ashington. But it meant I was on my own and, no matter how far away I was, the worry about my mam never left me. I was in a prison 5,000 miles away, surrounded by savage people, being told in a letter from my sister not to worry because mam would be all right. How could I be expected to take that information and just go, "OK, no problem"? It didn't work like that.

I felt like I had let myself down, and my family too. I should have seen the warning signs. My mam had been complaining about headaches for a while, and I just thought she was prone to migraines. Now I was beating myself up for ignoring her concerns. I should have told her to go the doctors. Why did I not insist that she went to get herself checked out?

After I received that shocking letter from Lisa, I walked all the way back to our cell feeling very down. All the while, I was getting abuse from Indian prisoners. They were shouting insults at me every step of the way. I felt I would explode and batter them. Instead, I just focussed. I tried to give myself tunnel vision so I wouldn't hear or see them. When I finally reached the cell, the first person I saw was Paul Towers.

Paul was not the biggest bloke, but he was a good three inches taller than me and leaner too as he worked out to keep in shape. He had shaved his head but grew a beard while we were in prison. Paul could be serious but, like a lot of army lads, he knew when to break the ice and have a laugh. Everyone was always under a lot of stress, missing their homes and families, so his friendship helped me to get through it all. He was a Liverpool fan, so we would make a brew, chat about football, then ask how things were with our families back home. It helped to talk about topics other than the case, and we were able to perk each other up during some very difficult times. That day, Paul could tell straight away that something was wrong. He took me off to one side and I broke down. I told him everything and said, "I can't do this. I need to go home, and I need to be with my family." He tried to comfort me, but what could he say? All he could really do was listen while I talked through my pain.

In that moment, if the Indian authorities had let me go home for a little while, I would have signed on the dotted line promising to come back, and I would have kept my promise. I would have given them my word, and I would have honoured it. I would have got back on a plane afterwards and returned to face the music. That was how much I wanted my family in that moment. But that was never going to happen.

I realised I had hit a very low point, but I shook my head clear and gave myself a good talking to. I knew I would have to deal with this latest blow somehow, as I had done with everything else. What choice did I have? Give up? Kill myself? No. I was battling with some dark thoughts, and I knew I had to completely change my approach to avoid descending into despair. I asked myself, "How do I move on from here?" I had to work through the options. It was the only way to avoid a dangerous spiral into depression.

I tried to think like a Para. I told myself that I had moved up a level, that I was facing a huge brick wall which I would need to conquer. This wall was mental, not physical, but I had to get over it just the same. I told myself I was not a quitter. That's not who I was. My experience in the Paras had shown time and again that I never gave up. I knew my mam would not want me to spend every minute out in Chennai worrying about her. I was one of the reasons she was trying to stay alive, and I couldn't let her down. She was fighting, and I had to be strong, too, for her sake and mine.

I made a promise to myself to be stronger, and I had every intention of honouring that promise.

Nights were often the worst. Sleeping in a prison wasn't easy. It was hot and the conditions were cramped, but it wasn't just the physical conditions that were the torment. At night, when everyone settled down to try to get off to sleep, we were left alone with our thoughts and, because of our circumstances, they were very often dark ones. There were times when I cried myself to sleep, and there were other nights when I couldn't sleep at all because my mind was racing. I was facing a really tough challenge, and it only became tougher when suddenly, and for no apparent reason, I stopped receiving any communication from home.

That was the lowest point during our first months in prison – when I didn't get a letter from my sister for nearly a month. It completely did my head in. I was the only one of the lads not getting letters and I couldn't understand why. The mail would come in, we would hand it round, and everybody would get something except me. Every day it was the same. It was like being a luckless kid, playing pass-the-parcel but never getting a prize.

Sharon, who would bring in the letters, could see that I was devastated. She understood the effect this was having on me. I could see the sadness in her face, and she could see it in mine. In the end, she said that she couldn't carry on like this, and she made a confession. "Nick, I am really sorry. I know why you have not been getting any letters, but I just couldn't tell you."

I couldn't imagine what had happened. I immediately assumed the worst. My thoughts went to my family and, in particular, my mam. Had something terrible happened to her?

"It was meant to be a secret, and I am not supposed to say," said Sharon. "But I have to tell you because I can't leave you feeling like this."

By now, I was fully fearing the worst. Then Sharon told me, "Your sister is coming to see you. Lisa is flying out from the UK to surprise you. That's why she didn't send you a letter. She's coming out here in person."

I almost broke down with a combination of relief, frustration and confusion. My sister had given up precious time and money to fly all the way out here to surprise her brother because she loved me that much. Keeping it a secret from me was the only part of the surprise I wish she could have changed. Lisa had the very best intentions, but she had no idea the impact of that long silence. How could she know what those letters meant? How could she begin to understand the paranoia and sadness that flooded in when I didn't hear from my loved ones for weeks? She wasn't in prison, and she could only imagine what it was like. She had no way of knowing why this lack of contact had floored me.

When Lisa did fly out for her first visit, in March 2014, it was wonderful to see her. She brought me some clothes, and it was great to have new T-shirts, vests, underwear and toiletries, all of which contributed to making me feel better. There was food from home too, including treats like biscuits and porridge. Lisa was brilliant, and she always tried to help the other guys as well. All the families were good like that. They never forgot the rest of the Chennai Six when they paid a visit to their loved ones. Every time a family member came over, they would try to bring whatever we needed.

Lisa's presence was a huge boost. She urged everyone to be happy and stay positive. She helped us to visualise the light at the end of the tunnel, even though some of us were struggling in the dark and it was hard to see a way forward. I had got the wrong end of the stick and thought she just hadn't bothered to write. I told her, "Please don't ever do that to me again." I was that upset. Of course, my poor sister didn't fully realise how that silence had ripped me apart. The last thing she wanted to do was make my life worse.

Looking back, it's amazing how I could endure so much that might have broken other men, but it was a simple thing, like not receiving a letter from home, that pushed me so close to breaking point. .

CHAPTER 20

NO STONE UNTURNED!

All the families back in Britain received communications from the Foreign Office. The people on the ground in India wrote up reports after every visit and sent them back to the UK. However, there were often delays. I thought that was because the officials in London weren't as proactive as those in India, although, ironically, Lisa thought it was the other way around.

We had the impression our government wasn't looking to force the issue, and ministers were happy to sit back and wait to see how it all played out. They assumed that, once the misunderstanding had been sorted, everything would come to a swift and happy conclusion, and we would be on our way home. I don't think the UK government realised the seriousness of our situation until we were convicted at the trial.

To begin with, there was the problem of the UK government failing to understand the nature of our case and our innocence. Ministers and officials didn't know the full facts, and it took us a while to convince them we had been genuinely stitched up. Also, they didn't want to make a lot of noise right at the beginning. They were hoping this would all blow over without any diplomatic row or adverse publicity. Another sticking point was the reluctance of the British government to declare publicly that we were innocent. Officials were hedging their bets. Because, if we went on to be convicted of something serious and we were sent to jail after receiving a loud endorsement from our government, the public would have been up in arms.

Most of the British public were very supportive, apart from a few typical keyboard warriors who thought we must be guilty of something and said so in their ill-informed social media posts. There are some sad people out there who like to wade in and make nasty comments just so they can spread their misery.

It took a lot of time to persuade those with the power that we were the victims of a miscarriage of justice, but we got there eventually. When we showed embassy officials the export licence for our firearms, which came from the Department of Business, Skills and Innovation – a UK government department – they started to understand what we were up against. Those guns had been in Mumbai one month earlier, and they had been accredited at that point. So how could they be illegal now? That made no sense, unless the farcical nature of the Indian judicial system was taken into account. If the police said up was down and black was white, the courts would believe them. Our Consulate guys passed on their concerns to British government officials, and they started to see we had been hard done by – although, even then, they still didn't fully comprehend the seriousness of our situation.

In February 2014, four months after we were first arrested and jailed, we received the charge sheet. Now, at last, we could finally read the case against us, including the laws the police claimed we had broken, and the full text of the charges. This was crucial because we would have to prepare a legal response to whatever the prosecution was about to throw at us.

In typical fashion, the charge sheet prepared by the Indian authorities was an absolute joke. It was farcical. There were only two charges against us, and they could have been written down on a side of A4 paper. Instead, we were presented with a charge sheet that was 2,158 pages long!

Of all the crazy things that had happened to us since we were hauled off the Seaman Guard Ohio, this was right up there with the daftest. The charges were so ridiculously long and absurdly detailed, they took up three volumes. Each of these large books was filled with completely pointless stuff, including every piece of irrelevant communication police had managed to intercept between the captain and the company. None of this had any bearing on our case at all.

When we went to the court to get hold of the charge sheet, every one of us was presented with a copy of all three of these massive books which contained the made-up fantasy they had concocted about us. Since there were 35 defendants, it meant they had to hand over 105 huge volumes of material.

When I received mine, I asked, "How many trees did you have to cut down to make that lot?" Later, I gave my copies to Lisa and told her, "Take them home and read them if you want to have a good laugh. It's all bloody fairy tales."

After we had waded into the documents, we managed to work out there were two areas where the police continued to claim we had broken the law. The first was the position of our vessel close to or, as they claimed, *within* Indian territorial waters. The second was the issue of the supposedly illegal weapons.

Our disputed position in their waters became a complicated aspect of our case, with claim and counterclaim about whether we had encroached on India's territory or not and, if we had, whether it even mattered because we weren't doing anything remotely illegal.

Their whole argument about the ship having entered territorial waters was undermined when it turned out the coastguard didn't know exactly where we were when they picked us up. They couldn't actually state our true position because the in-port navigation equipment wasn't working. At the very best, they could make a guess about our location and how close the ship was to shore, and even then, they certainly couldn't prove anything.

So how did they even find us, or know where we were in the first place? We were pretty sure someone had tipped off the authorities that we were closer to shore than we would normally have been. It was also possible that the mobile phone call from one of the officers on board the Seaman Guard had been intercepted, giving away our position.

The weapons charges should have been much simpler to dismiss because we had all the paperwork we needed to show that the guns were legal. These documents were simply ignored.

Back in Britain, there was shock that a supposedly friendly nation with deep, historic ties to Britain could treat us so badly. This was particularly true when some very high-profile political figures from the UK became involved in the campaign and still nothing was done to release us. You would have thought having all those household names on our side, supposedly lobbying for us, would make a big difference, but it didn't. India's government ignored all the pleas from the Foreign Office and did nothing to intervene in the case in Chennai. Perhaps, in a way, that showed how powerless we had become as a nation.

Our case was raised more than 50 times at ministerial level and nine times directly with Indian prime minister Narendra Modi, yet still nothing happened. My sister Lisa went on Victoria Derbyshire's TV show and said she was sick of hearing how our government couldn't directly interfere with another country's judicial process. That was the constant message she received from the Foreign Office.

We all thought we knew the real reason why the government wanted to tread lightly. There was an enormous trade deal in the offing, and no-one wanted to rock the boat before that was signed, sealed and delivered. A few imprisoned Brits were of secondary importance. If you maintain a belief that the British government would move heaven and earth to help a British citizen out of a jam in a foreign land then you are deluded, particularly if there is money involved. With a trade deal in the balance, ministers were never going to do much more than ask politely about our release if there was even the slightest risk that a stronger demand might cause offence.

During our years in Chennai, our case was raised by three foreign secretaries and two prime ministers to no great effect.

David Cameron, prime minister at the time of our arrest, at first seemed more worried about kissing Indian prime minister

Modi's arse than the fate of six of his citizens who were trapped in a foreign country without hope of release. However, when he received the petition supporting us, and he saw that it was signed by so many voters, something must have registered, because soon afterwards we were granted bail after six long months in jail.

William Hague was foreign secretary when we were arrested in 2013, and he didn't really involve himself in our case at all at the start. I knew he was a busy man, but I wondered how hard it was to pick up the phone and have a word with his counterpart in India to demand our release? To give him his due, he would later play a key role in our effort to get out of jail, at least until our case could be heard in a court of law.

When William Hague stepped down as foreign secretary, he was replaced by Phillip Hammond in July 2014. I can honestly say that, from my perspective, Hammond was a complete waste of space. He was foreign secretary for two years and in all that time I don't think he gave our case a single thought. From the outset, he gave the Chennai Six to junior ministers such as Hugo Swire, Alok Sharma and Mark Field. Maybe he thought we were a waste of his valuable time but, whatever the reason, it seemed like Hammond just couldn't be bothered to become involved.

Eventually it was the turn of possibly the most high-profile politician in Britain to oversee the Foreign Office. Boris Johnson stepped into the role of foreign secretary in 2016. He was appointed by the then prime minister, Theresa May, in an attempt to keep him on side during the Brexit fall-out. We hoped this supposed man-of-the-people would actually give a damn about our plight.

When he was asked about the case by one of his fellow Tory MPs in the House of Commons, he promised "to leave no stone unturned" in the effort to get us released. I think it would be fair to say that he left a lot of stones unturned. What did he do for us? Nothing, as far as I could tell. He was all mouth. Since Boris Johnson has become prime minister, a job he had always wanted, I have never believed a single word he said about anything.

Of all the politicians we dealt with, and there were a few if we counted all the ministers and Foreign Office officials, the one I had the most time for was Theresa May, who became prime minister after Cameron in 2016. I don't know if it was because she was a woman, but I believe she genuinely cared about us. In my opinion, women tend to be more sympathetic than men, even in politics, and she certainly took more of an interest in our plight than David Cameron or Boris Johnson ever did. May kept raising our case, even bringing it up with the Indian prime minister Modi at a G20 summit in November 2016, for what that was worth.

Our ministers all got it wrong, and I know exactly what should happen in future if the UK is going to avoid a terrible situation like ours from ever happening again. Government policy must change. Currently, the government waits until someone is found guilty before it intervenes. We were told that more could have been done for us after we were convicted but, of course, by then it would be way too late, the miscarriage of justice would already have happened. The Foreign Office should step in and start lobbying foreign governments hard when the evidence strongly indicates their citizens have done nothing wrong. It's much easier to have someone freed before they are tried and found guilty by a court of law.

Finally, our government should put the interests of its own citizens before trade deals. No-one should ever have to feel that people at the highest level are more worried about offending a foreign government than letting their citizens rot.

I had served my country as a soldier. I put my life on the line as a paratrooper in two war zones, and I had almost died in the line of duty for my Queen and country – but where was my country now? I have always been proud to be a member of an elite regiment of the British Army, but when I really needed the government on my side, it failed me.

* * *

Our government might have let us down, but we did get a hell of a lot of support from another British institution – the press. From the moment journalists learned of our plight, newspapers began campaigning for our release. Our faces were suddenly on the front pages of Britain's biggest selling tabloids. The Sun and the Daily Mirror made sure everyone knew there was absolutely no doubt about our innocence – and that really mattered to us. Everyone with a smartphone seemed to have an opinion about us, and they were not shy in voicing it. Endless internet trolls were free to call us mercenaries and gun runners, saying there was no smoke without fire. So the truth being told by the tabloids in big headlines was a huge deal for us.

The Sun and the Mirror were always behind us, and they made sure we had some very high-profile backers. Prince Charles was the colonel-in-chief of the Parachute Regiment and he gave us his support, as did his son Prince Harry, who was a soldier himself and a veteran of the Afghan war. His work founding the Invictus Games for wounded veterans showed how much he cared about former soldiers, and it was great to know he was on our side. We also received a message of support from actress Joanna Lumley, who famously campaigned to help members of the Gurkhas in their quest for a fair deal from the British government.

The British newspapers ran a series of stories about us, and their campaigns kept us in the public eye, helping to ensure we would never be forgotten. The publicity also kept pressure on government ministers because they knew the campaign would not let up until we were finally released. I will always be grateful for that.

Our local press did us proud too, with the Newcastle Chronicle running story after story on me and covering Lisa's campaign at home. They never forgot. It meant a lot to us knowing that, no matter how down we were in prison, there were so many people out there who knew and cared about us. It helped us to keep going.

CHAPTER 21

TWISTING THE KNIFE

After five months in prison, the prospect of bail started to look more likely. If nothing else, bail would mean an improvement in our living conditions. I'd still be stuck in India and forced to report to the police station every day, but at least I would have some freedom of movement. Bail wouldn't have been too much to ask for. We were innocent and the police knew it, but they were still determined to ensure our lives were as miserable as possible. They continued to press their bogus claim that our guns were illegal, and time after time they convinced the court to reject any bail application. For a long while, it seemed like we would never get out of prison.

At this point, my amazing sister played a key role in a campaign to get us released, a campaign that would eventually reach the prime minister, David Cameron. She, and the other families of the imprisoned men, had been pushing hard to get the case of the Chennai Six raised at the highest levels of the British and Indian governments. They realised that politicians only listened to, and cared about, a case like ours when it became a big national story. So the families started a petition, and momentum soon began to grow.

The case against us was complicated because it involved the technicalities of encroaching on India's waters – a subject outside the knowledge and experience of most people. Despite this, the families did a great job getting over a simple message that these men were innocent and there was absolutely no reason for them to be imprisoned abroad. If you signed this petition you were demanding that your government took more action to secure their release.

It worked, and the majority of the British public not only understood our plight but were appalled by it. The signatures started rolling in, and the numbers grew at an astounding rate. The aim was to get above 100,000 names so the petition would be taken seriously. That seemed like a hell of a task to begin with but, thanks to the tenacity of Lisa and the other families, word soon spread online and in the media about the forgotten Chennai Six, the British victims of a serious miscarriage of justice.

Lisa travelled down to London, met members of the other families, and went to Downing Street to ensure the petition was delivered right to the heart of government. Campaigners eventually gathered 136,000 signatures in all, and I can't express how much it meant to us to know we had such support from the public at large. It was incredible to think that so many people took time out of their busy lives to demand that the government lobby hard for our bail. It was wonderful, and it made a difference. I'm certain about that.

Despite this sense of momentum, the bail process itself was long and needlessly cruel. It took a strange turn when one of our jailers told us, "Don't worry. You are getting out in a couple of weeks." We weren't sure whether to believe him or not, but he made the claim with such conviction and authority that it sounded like our release was a done deal. We thought, he surely must know something. He seemed positive it was going to happen. Two more weeks then bail? We could cope with that. If we knew some kind of freedom was just around the corner, the time in between would become much more bearable. We were counting the days, and all the time the jailer was assuring us that bail, and our release, was getting closer and closer.

One day, that same jailer came to see us and told us exactly want we wanted to hear. Bail had finally been granted! We had been waiting for so long and we were so relieved. He told us to pack up our things because we were leaving immediately. Excited to get out of there, we quickly put all our stuff together and headed off. I couldn't wait to get beyond those prison walls.

Carrying our bags, we all trooped down to the office together where the prison officer would complete the paperwork, sign us out, and tell us the conditions of our bail. I was so happy.

When we arrived, the superintendent looked confused. "What are you doing?" he said. We explained the situation: that the jailer had told us we had been granted bail, and we were all getting out today. He looked at us as if we had gone completely mad. Then the penny dropped. There was no bail and no release. We weren't getting out. Our jailer had made up the whole story, maintaining his cruel joke for two weeks, right up till this last moment when release was, in our minds, within touching distance.

When we confronted the jailer, he denied everything. He claimed he had never said anything about bail. He had been taking the piss for weeks. The man had lied to us repeatedly right up until the moment he watched us pack our bags and troop to the exit, our spirits raised. He must have been beside himself with glee when he witnessed us walking back to our cells, absolutely devastated by the turn of events. It was mental torture for us, but he was having the time of his life.

I still can't explain why he did it, except that the man was a fucking idiot or "tapped in the heed", as we say where I am from. At the time, we thought drugs might have been a factor because he definitely acted as if he was taking something very strong. Who knows? In his head he might actually have believed we were getting bail. Either way, that episode was just one of a series of cruel acts played out at our expense while we were in India.

We started to get used to the lying. People did it all the time over there, and straight to our faces. It seemed second nature for them to lie to us about more or less everything. So much so that there was never any possibility of trust between us. The police lied routinely, otherwise we wouldn't have been there, and the people giving evidence in court lied, and nobody seemed to get pulled up on that. In British courts, that's the crime of perjury and it's a serious offence, often resulting in jail time. In India, it was just how things worked and barely merited a shrug from the judge. The lies continued pretty much all the time we were in prison. I used to tell the lads, "Everyone lies out here, everyone. You can't believe any of them." We used to say, "Out here, they can't even lie straight in bed."

For most of our time in jail, we heard virtually nothing from the lawyers or the court. We continued to hope that someone might see sense and, at the very least, grant us bail. How could we be a risk or a danger to anyone when no-one really believed we had done anything wrong?

We knew when we were supposed to make a court appearance, and we knew there were a lot of sureties to put in place to make sure we didn't run off but, other than that, we heard hardly anything from the legal side. We waited and waited.

In the usual chaotic fashion, the first we heard that we had been granted bail for real was from the Indian inmates of the prison. They had read the news in the paper. It was typical of the authorities to tell reporters the latest, but not to bother to share the information with us. Nobody came to tell us officially and when prison guards eventually did get around to informing us, we were still scarred from our previous false alarm, thanks to our mad jailer. We refused to believe the announcement until we saw something official or heard from someone with real authority.

Even when we were finally convinced that bail had been granted, it still took another 10 long and frustrating days to get us out of prison. That was how disorganised the system was. As we were foreigners in an Indian prison, bail was more complicated for the judicial system to handle than leaving prison for good. The police would need to set up a system to keep tabs on us all. Any hopes I had that I might be allowed to fly home to Newcastle and wait to be called back to India were quickly dashed. I suppose the police assumed we would never return – and they were right to think that.

By this stage, I had already served a six-month prison sentence despite having done nothing illegal. There were people in the UK who had committed all kinds of crimes, some involving violence, and they didn't get as much prison time as we had endured while waiting for the Indian authorities to make up their minds.

We waited and waited, and more days passed. What were they playing at? We had been granted bail on 26 March 2014, but it was 7 April before the prison finally opened its doors and allowed us to leave.

Even at this last minute, we didn't entirely trust prison officials to do the right thing. When the guards said we were leaving the prison, we didn't move. We stayed put. They were surprised by our reluctance, but they should have known better. By this time, they must have figured out we didn't trust a word anyone said to us any more. We told them we wouldn't move till the superintendent himself came down and told us in person. He was the only one we trusted to tell us the truth. When he eventually put in an appearance and confirmed the news, we finally acknowledged the fact we would soon be on our way. We quickly packed our stuff and headed to the entrance of the prison. This time, it wasn't a trick or a wind-up. The prison doors opened for us, and we were allowed to step into the outside world for the first time in six months. It wasn't exactly freedom but, in that moment, it felt as good as.

But there was a sting in the tail. Of the 35 men held for six months in that prison, only 33 of us could leave. Two of our group would not be going anywhere. The captain was denied bail because the authorities held him responsible for the position of the ship. The other poor bastard who had to stay put was Paul Towers. Investigators still thought, wrongly, he was second-in-command. He wasn't, of course, but they viewed him as the man in charge of the armed lads doing the anti-piracy work. He was therefore responsible for all the weapons that investigators claimed were illegal. They weren't going to risk letting him out. It was a cruel blow for Paul, and I could only imagine what was going through the poor guy's mind when he had to watch the rest of us walk out of prison without him.

They kept Paul and the captain for two more cruel and unnecessary months of interrogation. Paul was questioned over and over with his accusers drumming into his head that he was "a very bad man", even though they must have known they were spouting rubbish. If they were hoping that he would cave under pressure and admit to crimes he hadn't committed, they had picked the wrong man.

When we left prison, we were marched to buses that AdvanFort had organised for us. The Estonians were on one bus, and we went on another. By this time, news of the Chennai Six and this latest development in the saga had spread far and wide. We had become a big story. Though not everyone knew the full facts, most observers around the world understood that something very dodgy was going on in the Indian judicial system, and we were the victims, not the cause. We left prison to a chorus of sympathy.

Interest in our plight was strong enough to draw the media down to witness our departure. A TV crew from ITV gave each one of us a bottle of Coke. Even better, it was cold. There was no refrigeration in our prison, so this was fantastic. It was my first cold drink in six months. This small and simple act of kindness from the TV crew was hugely significant to us, and I will always remember the gesture. I'll also never forget the taste of that deliciously cold bottle of Coke. It was wonderful, like tasting heaven, and I guzzled it down.

We set off on the bus and our destination was a hotel. The Radisson Blu in Egmore, Chennai's city centre, would have been a very nice hotel in any circumstances, but after six months locked up in an Indian prison in appalling conditions, it felt like unimaginable luxury. Two of us shared a room, but that was fine because we were used to four of us being crammed into a much smaller space.

That first night, I had a lovely long shower and luxuriated in the hot water. There was plenty of it, and I could actually control the temperature. In the prison, the temperature of the water only varied with the season. It was warmer in the summer when the pipes heated up but that was it. There were no taps or levers to make it hotter or colder.

We did our interview with the TV crew, then we all met up and enjoyed some food and drink together in the hotel. I had my first beer in months. Like that bottle of Coke, it was cold and very refreshing, but I didn't want to overdo it. I knew we had to be up the next morning to report to the police station for the first time. I couldn't risk missing that vital appointment because I'd slept in or was suffering a hangover. They'd probably send me right back to prison again, and it would have all been for nothing.

The first meal outside the prison walls was great. I had a steak and it was lovely, the first really nice food I'd eaten in ages. My body reacted later though and... well, let's just say it went straight through me, and leave it at that.

You would have thought I would have slept like a log that night. I'd been very well fed and had a beer or two, I was lying in a nice bed with crisp, clean sheets, a soft pillow and a good mattress, and I was emotionally drained after a very big day. But it took me a while to fall asleep. I had been used to kipping on a thin mattress in a prison cell for six months. It was going to take a while to get used to comfort.

While I was in prison, I realised it was the simple things that I experienced in my everyday life that I missed the most. These days, I appreciate them more and more. Hot water and cold drinks, showers, pillows and clean sheets on my bed – I will never take any of them for granted again.

The next morning, we jumped into a hotel car and headed straight to the police station for our first sign-in. We had to be there for 10am and make the same trip in the evening for 8pm, every single day. It was a pain, but worth it to get a little taste of freedom. The police officers didn't talk to us because of the language barrier, but it was clear what we were supposed to do. There were little passport photos of each of us in books, like old school exercise books, and we had to sign against our pictures. As soon as they were happy that we hadn't done a runner, they let us get on with our day, for the next 10 hours at least, until we were back there again in the evening.

I felt I had some liberty, but it wasn't real freedom. We were always signing on at that police station, and we couldn't do much during the day in between our morning and evening appointments. We found ourselves clock-watching all day, and the worry was constantly at the back of our minds: what would happen if we missed a sign-in? Would they react badly and slam us back in jail again if we skipped one appointment, or showed up late? I couldn't risk that outcome, and I was never able to relax as a result.

We were pleased AdvanFort had finally stepped up and sorted out a nice hotel for us – and it was clearly a massive improvement on our previous living conditions. But we should have guessed it was too good to be true. We reckoned later that the company was putting on a show to make a statement to the world. It was a good PR exercise to demonstrate that AdvanFort was truly looking after its employees. That didn't last. It wasn't long before we were told by the hotel that the company was planning to stop funding our stay. AdvanFort was worth a lot of money, and the owner was a very wealthy man, but he wasn't going to pick up the tab for us to stay there for a prolonged period. We were soon on our way again. I had very low expectations by now but even I couldn't believe where we ended up.

CHAPTER 22

A NON-PERSON

AdvanFort was just like the Indian authorities in its love of secrecy. Company executives wouldn't tell us anything to our faces, and that even stretched to the nature of our living accommodation. We only learnt that the company was ending our stay at the Radisson Blu from the hotel management.

The company moved us to another hotel, but this was a hell of a comedown after four weeks in the Radisson Blu. The place was abysmal. Conditions were so bad, it almost felt as if we were back in prison again. I couldn't even touch the food, which was appalling. That's quite a thought after I had just spent six months eating the worst that a prison cook house could offer us. We could get rice and dahl in the hotel, but even the native Indians were turning up their noses at the dishes. They were dreadful, and I quickly realised I would have to buy all my food from outside.

It cost about £30 a week to stay in the hotel, which sounds very cheap, but it was over-priced taking into account the conditions. There was no hot water, and we were packed in three or four to a room. It would have been bearable as a normal, decent-sized hotel room with twin beds, but the hotel had squeezed two more camp beds into every room to pack in as many people as possible.

163

We stayed there from May right through till August, and guess what? The company ran up another bill that ended up not getting paid. The hotel wasn't happy. The manager started demanding money from each of us. He claimed there was a bill of £20,000 which needed settling. My share would have been £500, but I refused to pay. I hadn't been given any choice on where I wanted to stay. I had been placed there by the agent from the company. I would hardly have picked this rotten place if I had been given the option to go elsewhere. I heard that some of the lads were talking about paying up, but I was having none of it. My view was that the hotel's grievance was with the company not me. I packed up and left.

When we reported the problem to the consulate, officials said there was nothing they could do. Meanwhile, the Estonian lads contacted their embassy and things went very differently. Everything was sorted out for them. Estonian officials came down and told them, "Pack your stuff, you're leaving." They had found their lads alternative accommodation.

That decision worked out OK for me, too, in the short term. I ended up staying at the same place as two of the Estonian guys, Aivar and Alvar, as well as John from our group of Brits. We found a little hostel and managed to get one room for the four of us so we could keep the cost down. It wasn't all plain sailing though. With four guys living in such close proximity, tensions rose, and tempers flared. It was inevitable. Anyone stuck in circumstances like that, even with their very best friends, would soon be at each other's throats. We didn't have enough space or privacy, and arguments soon followed.

After a while, John decided to leave and go off on his own. That meant there was three of us left. Mostly, I just did my own thing and kept myself to myself during the day. Alvar and Aivar would go off for hours, walking here, there and everywhere, but that wasn't for me. I told them I didn't want to see any more of this shit-hole than I needed to. Instead, I used to go down to the shopping mall to experience a bit of civilisation. That was one way of escaping the dirt, grime and extreme poverty I would witness every day. People were literally pissing and shitting in the streets, and there were beggars everywhere.

It was a short journey by motorised tuck-tuck down to the nearest mall. The place was clean, and it had air con, which meant it was way better than my hotel. I could wander round and forget my crappy living conditions for a while.

The Estonians had the same money problems we were facing. They couldn't work, so they couldn't earn. There was one big and important difference though: they received money directly from their government. We didn't receive anything like that from ours. It always seemed strange to me that a small, not exactly rich country like Estonia would look after its guys much better than the government of the fifth richest nation on the planet.

In the end, I had a falling-out with the two Estonian lads which was caused by the time difference. When I wanted to speak to my sister, I would have to wait until she finished work at 7pm in the evening, UK time. Unfortunately, that was about 2am our time. My phone would bleep with a message in the middle of the night as a signal, and then I would take the call in the corridor outside while trying not to disturb my room-mates. I wasn't always successful. One day, Aivar took exception to my night-time calls. He got the serious hump in fact and started lashing out at me. Things looked like they were about to get serious with the likelihood of a proper punch-up, but Alvar managed to get between us, and he broke it up.

Once again, the Estonian government came to our rescue when they found the two lads a little bungalow somewhere. Off they went. I certainly don't hold any grudges against John, Aivar, Alvar, or any of the other lads for any fall-outs we might have had along the way. Tensions ran high because of the conditions we were forced to live in and the pressures we were under. We couldn't have expected anything else under the circumstances. Occasionally, tempers would erupt, but it didn't mean anything in the larger scheme of things. I'd still say hello to them if I saw them again. We were all in this together.

Now, I was truly on my own. I barely encountered any of the others from that point. We might bump into each other every now and then, but that was a rare occasion. I was getting on with my life, such as it was, and I wanted to tackle this next chapter in a positive frame of mind. I didn't mind too much that I was doing this in isolation. In a way it was easier. I could focus on keeping myself strong, physically and mentally. We had all been through a hell of a lot together, so maybe it was better we had some time away from each other for a while. It was healthy, in fact.

Once I was up each morning, I would take a shower, then nip out and get something to eat. Every day it was a challenge to fill the hours positively and not dwell on my situation. Somehow, I managed to get just enough cash coming in to scrape by. Money was sent out to me by my family, and a couple of friends would put money in my account. The ABF, the Army Benevolent Fund, Royal British Legion and the Parachute Regimental Association helped too. The Mission To Seafarers was great. Their people focused on helping the families back home because they were struggling too. My sister had to pay some of my credit card bills because the banks weren't interested in postponing my debts, even though she explained I was stuck in India and unable to earn any money.

Getting even half-decent food was always difficult, and I was always glad of the fast food franchises that operated out there. I became very familiar with the Domino's Pizza franchise in Chennai, and Papa John's. There were also McDonald's and KFC, but they were different from the ones back home. Money-wise, I had just enough to survive on and live some sort of a life. I'm not going to hide the fact that I went out drinking from time to time too. If that sounds irresponsible, I think it was justified under the circumstances. If I didn't go out occasionally, I would have gone mad. No-one could spend a year-and-a-half, day in, day out, sitting in a crappy hotel room just staring at the walls. Anyone who tried would be certain to sink into a depression.

I would reach the point where I couldn't bear sitting in that grotty room at the weekend, so I would go out for the evening. The best places to drink were the hotel bars, because they were smarter than the local dives. I would occasionally meet people and get chatting. I'd talk to foreigners who were there for work. I became friendly with a group of Irish workers, and these guys eventually asked me what I was doing in India. I never lied. I always told people the truth about my situation. Why not? I had nothing to be ashamed of. I said I'd been arrested and imprisoned and now I was out on bail. I was going through a difficult time, but I was entirely innocent. They were taken aback, and I could see their eyes widen, wondering who this person was they were talking to.

I could tell when someone was sceptical about me and my story. I couldn't say I blamed them. They were probably wondering if I really was innocent. If that was the case, they were thinking, how come he had been arrested, jailed and bailed? There was no smoke without fire after all. It didn't help that virtually all the foreign criminals I met while I was in prison were on charges relating to drugs offences. At least I could tell my new bar mates to type my name into Google and read all about me online. I could point to plenty of press coverage on the web about us and highlight the huge campaign to free us. There was even a Facebook page, set up by my sister, entitled "Help Nick Home". Once anyone checked out those pages, they understood and started to relax.

I didn't suggest that anyone should scan the local, Indian press to find out any useful information though. Their reports were an absolute joke. According to the local papers, we were highly dangerous gun runners who were looking to supply terrorists. Apparently, our plan was to sell weapons to the infamous guerrilla separatist group the Tamil Tigers so they could stage a Mumbai-style attack on the Kudankulam Nuclear Power Plant, 430 miles to the south. We had apparently been caught in the nick of time by plucky, local police officers who were the true heroes of the story. No prizes for guessing who told them all that!

It was Q Branch who kept the Indian press briefed with this torrent of outrageous lies. People talk about fake news a lot these days, but that's usually to be found online. In Chennai, I would see it in the newspapers every day, and most of it came directly from the authorities pushing their own agenda. Every time we had a court appearance, the Indian press would gather to hear the latest. The police couldn't reach them quick enough afterwards to spin their bullshit and feed them the line to take. In the meantime, we were silenced by our lawyers, who told us not to speak to the press, as if that could make the situation any worse than it already was.

Now we had a little taste of freedom, we wanted more of our old life back. When we were first taken off the ship and arrested, we were forced to leave all our belongings behind. The authorities would never let us go back on board to collect them. Now we were out of prison, we all reckoned life would be a hell of a lot better if we could reclaim our personal items. But still the authorities wouldn't allow us. All our gear had been left on the Seaman Guard Ohio for months. It was our stuff and we hadn't been convicted of any crime, but still they wouldn't permit us to collect our own belongings. It was typical obstructive behaviour.

Like everything in India, this situation dragged on for ages. It took the authorities a year before they finally sent word to us that we would be allowed to go back to the ship. There was no reason at all for this delay except to wind us up and make our lives more difficult than they needed to be. Talk about petty. If you think I am exaggerating about how mean-spirited and small-minded they were, then what happened on the day of our return should be evidence enough.

We had to travel for nine hours by road to get all the way back to Tuticorin port where the ship was berthed. That's the same as driving from the south of England all the way up to the Highlands of Scotland. Still, the journey was going to be worthwhile, because I had an iPod, a mobile phone and laptop waiting for me there, assuming, of course, no-one had nicked them.

With our classic bad luck, we all piled down there on the hottest day of the year, with temperatures well above 40C. It was the kind of weather that would keep normal people indoors because it was too damned hot to move. We were all burning up, but the police would not let us seek shade anywhere. Instead, they made all 30-odd of us wait outside at the port beneath a scorching sun. Even though we had brought plenty of liquid, the water soon either evaporated, or became so hot it was almost bubbling in the bottles. We were all severely dehydrated and suffering serious sunburn, but the Indian police didn't care. On the contrary, they were loving it.

We just wanted to collect our things as quickly as possible and get out of there. We still had a nine-hour drive back. Of course, the police were never going to make it that simple for us. Not when they could have their fun. The bastards made us wait outside, in the fierce heat, with no shade for 14 hours – 14 hours! – before they finally let us on board. It was a cruel and completely unnecessary delay, and they only did it so they could sit in their air-conditioned 4x4s and laugh at us.

The only upbeat note was when I discovered my stuff was intact, providing me with a valuable lifeline to my family and the wider world.

When I finally returned to my hotel, the round trip had taken a colossal 32 hours. I was so exhausted, dehydrated and sunburnt. I went to bed and slept for nearly two days. It was a completely soul-destroying exercise, and the only reason it happened was because of the pure spite of the police who relished watching us suffer.

Enduring that miserable journey was worth it in the end because I was finally able to speak to my family and friends online. That gave me valuable and frequent contact with loved ones. That was so important to me because, while I was on bail, I couldn't really do anything. I wasn't allowed to leave the city, let alone the country. I couldn't work, so I wasn't able to earn any money. The police continued to insist that we signed in twice a day at the station, so I went through the same routine every day between April and July 2014. After that, and until our conviction in January 2016, I was in limbo. An innocent man but not free. I felt like a non-person.

While the legal case rumbled on and we awaited trial, there was always a troubling thought at the back of mind that I might never be allowed to leave India. I was worried sick about that outcome. The prospect of a guilty verdict and a long prison sentence hung over me all that time and, as it turned out, I was right to be worried.

At one point I went to the British Consulate and explained I had no way to earn a living. I asked if they could help me with a grant or a loan, but they turned me down flat. When I asked them how I was supposed to live, officials told me I would have to rely on friends and family. It wasn't their problem. It was a good job I actually did have family and friends because, without them, pretty soon I would have been homeless and starving. While the Estonians on my ship were given money to live off by their government, I received no help from mine. My country, the one I had proudly served and fought for in two conflicts, didn't help me at all.

I was forced to live off handouts from friends, family and army charities, all of which chipped in at various points during my nightmare in India. If it wasn't for them, I don't think I would have been able to go on. Now my family are in debt because of me. That might not be my fault, but it doesn't make me feel any better about it. I have to live with the guilt of knowing they are still struggling because of me. I came home with nothing and, although I am now working, I received no compensation from anyone, not the Indian government, and certainly not my own. I can't understand why my country turned its back on me. Even a loan from the consulate would have been a lifeline. I'd far rather be in debt to my country than my family.

Of course, not every moment on bail in Chennai was terrible. I tried to make the best of my situation, and I learnt how to kill time in a positive way. I went to the gym every day and kept myself occupied. I lived in a cheap hotel that was very basic, but at least I had a room to myself. I bought an electric stove to cook food in my room and a kettle so I could brew up. There was even a little telly. I paid an extra quid a month so I could watch the English Premier League. The time difference meant I had to watch matches in the middle of the night, but it was worth it. I'm a Man Utd fan and when they played Man City in the derby, I must have got carried away because people came to investigate the noise. They thought I was beating someone up in my room because I was effing and blinding so loudly.

If I thought my luck in India couldn't get much worse, I soon got a brutal reminder that it could. It was Boxing Day 2014, and the local police were about to show me exactly how.

I used to go to a local bar to watch the football and have a few pints. That day, Man Utd beat Newcastle United 3-1 and, if I'm honest, I'd drunk more than a few. I was walking back to the hotel, and I stumbled past a police checkpoint. They saw an inebriated foreigner and demanded to see my papers. Of course, I didn't have any, but that was their country's fault not mine. I tried to explain to them that I had no papers, but that did not go down well. I kept repeating, "Q Branch have them", but they either didn't understand me or wouldn't believe what I was saying. By this point, there were four of them around me, and none of them understood the situation. After a while I just thought, "Fuck this, I am away." I told them, "I'm going back to my hotel." Then I tried to leave. Wrong move. My legs were knocked out from under me, and I hit the ground. I was dragged along a hard, gravel surface with lots of tiny stones, and these guys were not being gentle. By the time they were done, I was pretty badly injured. I thought I'd ripped the rotator cuff in my shoulder joint, and I ended up with a massive gash in my hand as well as a bad scrape all down my arm.

The police put me in a van and drove off. I was sitting there in a right mess, thinking this could end very badly, particularly if the police followed their usual practice and made up a bunch of false allegations about me. The police could have said anything they liked about why I was in such a state, and there wasn't much I could have done about it. If they decided to claim I'd assaulted one of their number, I'd be in even more trouble.

They sat me on a bench outside the police station and brought out the most senior officer available. He asked me why I didn't have any papers. They still didn't really understand me, but I kept saying, "American ship." I figured they might have heard of the Seaman Guard Ohio, as it was big news out there. I told them to "get Q Branch", until finally the penny dropped. They must have called someone at CID and informed them I was injured because, suddenly, not only was I released, but they drove me back to my hotel.

The next day, I went to a local doctor, and he had to use tweezers to get all the bits of gravel out of me. The wound was infected as well, so he injected me with iodine. As I suspected, I'd damaged my shoulder, and I couldn't go to the gym for weeks – and that was one of the few things I enjoyed. I was incapacitated, but at least it was my right hand and arm that took the brunt, and I am left-handed.

Following the assault, my injuries took a while to heal, and I was having a hard time. I didn't go out, and I got very down in the dumps. I was thinking, I can't do this any longer. I was on the phone crying to my dad and sister because I was in such a bad way. I realised I needed to go out and socialise again or I'd go mad, but my family were worried that I might cross the police again. I promised I wouldn't cause any trouble.

One night in July 2015, I went out to a bar where westerners and Indians were mixing together. There, I met a girl. She spoke good English, and I learned her name was Monalisa Das. I thought she was really nice, and good looking too. She told me she had booked a taxi to take her somewhere else, and she left. It was typical of my luck because I really liked her. I had no time to feel sorry for myself though because she quickly returned. She told me she'd cancelled her taxi so we could carry on talking. Maybe my luck was changing after all. Later, we went off to a nightclub and had a great time. I started seeing her after that.

Over the next few months we spent a lot of time together. Monalisa was very kind, always nice and loving. She used to mimic Geordie slang words and had a good sense of humour. Even her accent changed, and she started to speak a bit like me. We had some good times. We would go out for food and drink and went on dates. This was great for me because nothing else was going well, and it took my mind off my situation for a while.

Monalisa and I were in a relationship for six months, up to the point when I was given that long prison sentence. I fully expected her to give up on me, but she never did. I told her I did not expect her to stay with me, but she kept in touch, even though I was facing a long time behind bars.

She tried to visit me in prison a couple of times a week. It was rarely easy. Sometimes she would have to wait for up to nine hours in the direct sun before being turned away by the guards. It took two months before the prison would grant her access, and that only came after Lisa had lobbied the Foreign Office to pressure the prison.

She would bring family letters in for me and would inform the other families that she was going to visit. She would then bring messages into the prison from them to give to their imprisoned relatives, and she would take messages out to send back to the families. She brought in gifts for me too, like extra food and books, and she didn't have to do any of that. It was so kind of her.

In any normal situation, we probably could have made the relationship work, but my lengthy prison term wasn't even the biggest obstacle we faced. That turned out to be the distance between our two countries. I was always going to come home eventually, and I would have never been able to settle in India after what I had been through. It wouldn't be fair on Monalisa to ask her to leave her family, friends and home to travel all the way to the north east of England to be with me.

The time difference didn't help. We hardly got the chance to speak. I finally realised how difficult it was to be in a relationship with a woman who lived so far away. I had no choice but to end it. I knew it was for the best, but I think it did break her heart. I really regret that. I wish things could have worked out differently with Monalisa, but circumstances were just too difficult. We had strong feelings for each other, and she will always have a place in my heart.

So, yes, there were some good times in among all the low moments. I got pally with the gym guys, and I wasn't always in a state of fury. Even so, there was no escaping the dark clouds on the horizon. I had spent a year-and-a-half waiting for the Indian legal system to grind slowly towards a point where they could be bothered to grant us justice. When it finally came, it wasn't the kind I was looking for.

CHAPTER 23

LISA'S STORY: JUST A GIRL FROM ASHINGTON

The families of the men arrested in Chennai were all in touch with each other early on, and within the first couple of weeks we held several meetings to consider what action we should take. Our priority was to secure the men's release at the earliest possible opportunity, but we didn't have much of a clue how to go about achieving that. Our first idea was to launch a petition urging the Indian government to release these clearly innocent men. We all agreed this seemed like a good starting point, with the Estonian families on board too. But, in the end, it just didn't work. To begin with, the public in the UK couldn't understand why we were petitioning a foreign government. We realised they had a point – Indian politicians didn't give a damn.

We were all so naïve back then. The families were shocked and traumatised by what had happened to their loved ones. We'd all been thrown into this madness, and none of us knew what we were doing. It felt like we were groping around in the dark.

It was clear that our petition wasn't strong enough. It had no hook, and we needed more than just a plea to the Indian government to release 35 men of different nationalities. A couple of months later, we tried again. We changed the petition so that it was directly aimed at the UK government. British ministers and officials were the ones who needed to lobby the Indian government to free the men. It brought the story closer to home and, crucially, the public could understand the issue more easily.

We set up a Facebook page alongside the new petition, and that forced us into a tough choice. We decided we had to focus solely on the six British lads, and not the other foreign nationals in prison with them. I felt bad, but we knew we had to be ruthless. It was the only way to make the media, the politicians, and the public sit up and take notice. It worked too. Word started to spread that six British military veterans had been wrongly imprisoned in India, and the lads started to receive a lot more coverage. This led to increased sympathy for their situation and more support for their release. That was what we desperately needed. We felt bad about not being able to include the Estonian lads as well, but we reasoned that if we could get one of the men home, we could get them all home. From that point onwards the British veterans became instantly recognisable as the Chennai Six. That was an important breakthrough for us because it energised the campaign for their release.

I wrote to the prime minister and the foreign secretary countless times. Their staff and secretaries must have thought, "It's that bloody woman from Ashington again." I'm normally a person who avoids confrontation – I'm a people-pleaser who rarely complains about anything – but I realised I would have to battle to get this case raised at a national level. It terrified me to get involved to that extent, but I knew there was power in people. If we could just get enough of them on our side, then surely the politicians would have to take notice. We had the whole of the north east with us, but we needed the rest of the country too. We needed to make some noise.

I knew the prime minister and Foreign Office would have piles of pressing matters on their desks, but this was my brother. I was not going to stop talking about his case until someone did something. I would not stop till the whole world knew about Nick and he was on his way home.

In my literally hundreds of letters to government, I never made any demands. That would have got me nowhere. Instead, I begged and pleaded with officials and ministers, and appealed to their better natures to intervene with the Indian authorities. They did do that, and they kept reassuring me it was at the top of the agenda, but nothing happened in response. We kept urging them to be stronger and more direct in their dealings. I used to tell officials that I understood that they did not want to upset a foreign nation, but they could still demand that these innocent men were returned. We asked to see exactly what they had said when they raised the issue with Indian officials, but they wouldn't show us. We were not privy to that information, and they refused to give us even the smallest proof that they were pursuing this with anything like the drive we wanted. It left us with a deep suspicion that the government was still being too weak. We requested that the families of the Chennai Six meet with our prime minister, David Cameron, but that was ignored with no reason given. We were told No. 10 was "aware of the situation and it's being looked into" but that was all. It was incredibly frustrating.

Ian Lavery genuinely cared. Our local Wansbeck MP arranged a meeting for mam and me with the shadow foreign secretary Emily Thornberry. She was fantastic and really engaged with us. She was far more interested than Boris Johnson when he was foreign secretary. He said he would leave "no stone unturned", but he did absolutely nothing. I lost my temper in the end, and I told the newspapers that Boris Johnson was all talk. I said the only thing at the top of Boris Johnson's agenda was Boris Johnson. All he cared about was himself. Funnily enough, I am not the only person who has taken that view of our current prime minister.

If it was possible, AdvanFort was worse than the UK government. From the beginning, it was clear the company management didn't give a damn about the men. It seemed to us, all AdvanFort executives cared about was reclaiming their ship.

AdvanFort hired a lawyer in India. Dr Thushara James worked hard and did a great job. Back in Britain, Stephen Askins, a specialist maritime lawyer, was hired by the company to liaise with Thushara out in India. He did a fantastic job too, and together they were both instrumental in helping Nick's case. Shockingly, I'm not sure either of the two lawyers was ever paid by AdvanFort. They helped the families with legal work for four years, then the company turned its back on them, and us. It was a disgrace. They were owed thousands of pounds for their work. The final sum was too much for us to pay them from the money donated by the public.

Both of them eventually had to stop working on the case for financial reasons and weren't involved in the trial. When the men were eventually convicted, Stephen felt so strongly about the injustice that he became involved with us again, even though he knew we couldn't pay him. He worked pro bono on the case as we pursued an appeal. This amazing man worked for nothing to try to get the lads freed. He has no idea how eternally grateful to him we will be for the rest of our lives. Stephen helped to save 35 men, and he did it for nowt. His work on the case went on for months, then years, and he was routinely bombarded with media queries. His interviews were excellent. He simplified a complex and difficult issue for those who didn't understand maritime law, and he managed to get our message across to the public and the people who mattered at key points. I don't know what we would have done without him.

After the conviction, we had to plead with Thushara to return to work on the appeal. We were forced to raise funds to pay her for her work and bring her back on board. Thanks to AdvanFort's billionaire owners, we had to resort to begging. That was how we raised the money to pay an Indian lawyer to bring my brother home. I have no words to describe how evil the owners of AdvanFort were. They had no heart. To my mind, they were not even human.

The UK government and AdvanFort both failed us, but the media was hugely supportive, and it made such a difference. When Ian Lavery stood up in parliament and talked about the men, their profiles were immediately raised. The story was picked up by ITV Tyne Tees when reporters realised Nick was from their patch. Initially, BBC Look North (North East & Cumbria) didn't seem to want to report the story, but once they saw the injustice they really got behind the lads. However, I featured a lot on BBC Radio Newcastle from early on in the campaign.

I was just a girl from Ashington. I had never done anything involving the media before, and I always found it incredibly nerve-racking. This was so far out of my comfort zone, it felt like I was living in a parallel universe. The last thing I wanted to do was go on the radio or the TV, but I knew I had to, for Nick's sake.

Whenever I made media appearances, I was always very aware of the sensitivities of the other families, and that made interviews even more tricky for me to negotiate. We were all different people and didn't always have the same outlook regarding the press. Half the families wanted to use the media and the other half did not. I firmly believed we needed to use the radio, TV and newspapers to tell as many people as possible about the massive injustice Nick and the other men were facing. The only way to get politicians to care was to make some noise. I argued that, if we kept quiet, the men would be forgotten, and no-one would bother to lift a finger to get them out. Most politicians only responded to pressure and that was what we needed to create. We couldn't do that without the media.

Some of the other families had a different view, which I respected and understood, even if I disagreed with their stance. They were worried that putting *the men in the public eye and turning the case into a major international incident could prove counter-productive. And some had children, and perhaps they didn't want to expose them to the glare of the publicity.*

Like I said, I understood those points of view, but I did not agree. No way was anyone going to stop me from talking about my brother's situation to anybody who would listen. He was sleeping on a concrete floor every night in a prison thousands of miles from home. Of course, I was going to shout about it. I remember thinking, "Don't dare tell me I couldn't do this."

Over the next four years, it seemed like I was always doing something with the media. I never got used to it. Every single one of those interviews was a nightmare. I was always so aware of the need to get the correct message across about Nick and the rest of the men, and I would always review my performances afterwards with a very critical eye. It didn't matter if friends or family members told me I had done well, I would still be sitting there beating myself up, thinking, I should have said this, or I should have said that. I was never happy. It was ridiculous and extremely stressful. I would look at the other campaigners and think, "They are so calm. Why am I always so anxious?" It almost became an obsession.

I felt the pressure more intensely because I was not just speaking for myself. I was also speaking for my brother, who wasn't around, and for my mam, who had no voice. I felt like I was fighting for my brother's life and for my mam's as well, because she needed our Nick home if she was ever going to get better.

As time went on, I started to have a strange feeling that I was actually beginning to need the media – and not just to help get Nick released. It was a kind of therapy. I couldn't make our government do anything and I couldn't influence the situation in India. Dealing with the press was the only thing I had any control over. I made sure reporters never had to chase me for information, and

I was always really open with them. I gave them everything. As much as I was incredibly nervous about interviews, to the point where I would be shaking with anxiety beforehand, I also found my relationships with the media therapeutic. I grew incredibly close to some of those reporters over time. They became part of my life. They came to my home to find out the latest developments in Nick's case, and it was comforting to know that they cared. I knew it was their job to report about a story and to be sympathetic and empathetic to get the best out of me, but that didn't matter. I needed to be comforted by them, and I latched onto them as if they were family.

It helped that the same people covered Nick's story for years, and they genuinely believed in his innocence. One young reporter, Charlotte Murphy (now Charlotte Elmore), worked for Metro Radio, and this was one of her first stories. She followed it every step of the way until she moved to Manchester for a different job with the same media company. She told me that, when Nick was finally released, she would come back and cover the story. She was so invested in his fate, she had to see it through to the end no matter what.

We did newspaper features in the Daily Mail and Daily Telegraph, and we were constantly in touch with north east correspondents for the Daily Mirror and The Sun. Our local paper in Newcastle, the Chronicle, was phenomenal. The team really got behind Nick every step of the way.

I went on national television three times. I appeared on Victoria Derbyshire's show, and that was a whole new level of nerve-racking for me. As I looked around the studio and saw all those cameras, I began to convince myself I was going to swear on live TV. I was constantly swearing at home due to the stress and frustration of Nick's ordeal in India. It was just raw emotion. And when I recorded radio interviews, I often had to do 10 or more takes because I would ruin them with my swearing. I was terrified I was going to do the same thing on Victoria's live show. I was telling myself, "Don't swear Lisa, don't swear, please don't say shit or bollocks." That just made it worse. And I knew my friends and work colleagues would be watching which also added to the pressure.

There were seconds to go before the interview, they were counting us in, and I was thinking, "What the hell am I doing here? I am just a girl from Ashington." I knew who to blame, of course, and I remember thinking, if our Nick ever does get home, he is in serious trouble because I am going to fucking kill him!

The interview started and as soon as the questions began, I managed to give my honest opinion, from the heart. My nerves settled, I came through it and, most importantly, I did not fucking swear!

No matter how uncomfortable I felt about doing interviews, I knew they were necessary. I had to force myself out of my comfort zone. It was exhausting. Whenever there was a new development with the case, I had 20 media contacts to phone to let them know. It was draining to repeat myself over and over, but there was no other way. Sometimes I would say to dad or Paul, "Can you not do it for once?"

They would just say, "But you're better at it and they know your face."

I would say, "Yes, and soon they'll be sick of seeing my bloody face."

If I'd had any choice, I wouldn't have done any media work. This was a painful and very personal ordeal. But there was no choice if I was going to help Nick. Colleagues would hear I was going to London to do a TV interview, and they would tell me how exciting they thought it all was — but I didn't find it exciting, not one bit. I faced constant anguish turning a private family matter into a public concern.

The trolls didn't help. Whenever I went on TV, or did a piece online with the newspapers, they would pop up and leave their spiteful comments.

I would read them and just feel sick. I was cold, apparently, and didn't care. Or I was too whiny or irritating because I was always crying and whinging on. It was sad to think that there were people out there who could see someone else break down in tears on television because they were desperately worried about a loved one and their only response was to find them irritating. What kind of people must they be to think like that?

Others would not believe the facts of the case. "Oh, for God's sake," they would say. "Her brother is guilty. Why can't she just accept it and move on?"

Some people said I should be imprisoned along with Nick because I was obviously a drug dealer sending steroids to him. After we were interviewed by Kay Burley on Sky News, following Nick's release, his appearance caused a bad reaction from some of the trolls. They expected my brother to look painfully thin, but, while in prison, he had managed to eat reasonably well under the circumstances, and he had stayed strong and fit. Because he was bulky, the trolls reckoned he had to be on steroids, and I must have been his dealer. It was ludicrous.

I became paranoid with that level of scrutiny, and I lost weight through stress and worry. But, no matter how nasty or hurtful the comments became, I never engaged with them. I was so exhausted, I didn't have the energy. When the trolls accused me of enjoying the TV limelight, I used to wonder why they couldn't they see the truth – that I was so tired of this? I barely had the energy to update my own Twitter feed, let alone argue with them all.

Thankfully, for every negative comment posted, there were usually 10 or 20 positive ones defending Nick. The good people vastly outnumbered the bad, and it was great to see the trolls getting shot down by normal, decent folk who put them firmly in their place.

The trolling did affect me though. It reached the point where I didn't want to go out in case I met one of them. Every time I left the house people would stop me in the street and ask about Nick. They were nearly always lovely, but I was constantly worried that, one day, I might meet someone who wasn't. I became incredibly paranoid, and I used to walk around with my head down so people wouldn't notice me.

I am single and, before Nick was jailed, I was open to the idea of dating someone, but I had no time for that while we were campaigning for his release. If I had met someone, I would have had to explain the whole story to them. My day job was demanding, and I was training for half-marathons. With my mam so ill and Nick stuck in India, I didn't have the time, energy or inclination to go out with anyone. In the end, I made a conscious decision to put my personal life on hold. People said I should have done the opposite – get on with my own life – but how could I?

I couldn't even go out for the night to take my mind off the situation because I carried the burden with me wherever I went. I would feel guilty that I was enjoying myself while Nick was suffering in prison. I used to wonder if people would look over at me and think, "Well, she's not bothered about her brother. She looks happy enough." Not that there was much danger of anyone seeing me laughing or smiling, because I never really felt that carefree. If I did go out, I didn't enjoy myself. I felt genuinely miserable.

Even when I met lovely, well-meaning people it was difficult just to have a chat because, understandably, they wanted to ask me about Nick. I would have to explain the whole saga to them from the beginning. It was exhausting, and I felt too tired to leave my home. In the end I stopped going out completely.

CHAPTER 24

CHARGES QUASHED

We were in regular communications with our lawyers, and they took our case to appeal to the High Court in Madras for us. As luck would have it, foreign secretary William Hague was planning a trip to India at the same time. He was Nick Simpson's local MP, in Richmond, Yorkshire, so we hoped he would have an extra incentive to become involved and put in a good word on our behalf. We thought he could provide some influential support if the Indian authorities in Delhi were in the mood to co-operate.

We finally heard he was due to visit India in July 2014, and he might be prepared to raise our plight with the Indian government. We hoped he would press hard to have us freed. Surely, all it would take at that level was a quiet word with his opposite number. Like everyone else, Hague must have known we had done nothing wrong.

He arrived in India on Monday 7 July and was scheduled for a meeting on the Wednesday. He raised our case, then left on Thursday. Sure enough, on the Thursday word came through that all the charges had been quashed. We still don't know what he said but it had the required effect. On 10 July 2014, Justice P N Prakash of the High Court in Madras threw out all the charges. We were ecstatic.

I was in the gym at the time and one of the Indian crew members came in and told me. He said. "It's been quashed. It's over."

I thought, "That's champion!" and I went off looking for Ray to tell him the great news.

This was four months into our time on bail, and it felt very significant indeed. The High Court must have been deeply unimpressed by the prosecution argument because the court had thrown out the whole thing. Our charges had suddenly disappeared, and it seemed that justice had finally been done – even if it was very late in coming.

There were still some charges outstanding against the captain and chief engineer of the ship. These related to the fuel and the way it had been brought on board but, crucially, the weapons offences had been dropped. It looked like most of us were in the clear. I allowed myself to think that our nightmare might finally be coming to an end.

At that moment, because there were no longer any charges outstanding against us, we should have been given back our passports. We should have been free to leave the country forever. I should have been allowed to go home. But the Indian authorities disregarded their own laws and kept us in the country, detaining us unlawfully. We were informed that the police had the right to appeal this latest verdict and had 90 days to lodge their objections. We were all hoping they would finally see sense and let this one go, but, based on our experiences so far, I strongly doubted it would work out so smoothly. I had a very strong suspicion the police would fight the court's decision till the very end.

We wanted to set up a meeting with the consulate as soon as possible so we could press officials to claim our passports back and we could go home. Not long after the ruling, an official from the Deputy High Commissioner's office travelled down from New Delhi, and we had a meeting with her. We had letters from our lawyer stating that, according to Indian law, we didn't have to stay in the country during the 90-day period in which the police could lodge an appeal. This was the opportunity we had been waiting for. It seemed the perfect time to lobby the Indian authorities to let us go. If I had my passport back, I would have been on the first plane out of there. There was no way I would hang around for another three months, waiting to find out whether the police were vindictive enough to appeal against the decision to quash the charges.

For some reason, our embassy didn't see it the way we did. UK officials just didn't have the same sense of urgency or foreboding as we did. We tried to impress upon them that this was an important window, but we would have to move quickly before it slammed shut. Instead, the attitude seemed to be that we should all just wait and see what transpired. The embassy thought the police wouldn't bother to appeal. Officials reasoned that it was better to avoid causing a row by applying pressure when the alternative was simply to let the clock run down. After 90 days we would be free anyway, so what did it matter if they didn't give us our passports until then?

This was crazy thinking. I kept trying to tell them the police *would* appeal. No way would Q Branch want to back down and end up looking stupid. Q Branch knew its credibility was on the line, so this was a case of all-or-nothing for them. Its officers would do everything they could to keep us there. We urged the embassy to be more proactive on our behalf – but all our pleading fell on deaf ears.

Eighty-eight long days passed out of the 90 that Q Branch had been granted to appeal against the verdict. We were just two days away from freedom when, with typical vindictiveness, an appeal was lodged. No way were we going to be allowed to leave now.

I had seen this coming, and I was truly pissed off. I was angry at the police and angry at our embassy which did not push to get our passports back and see us safely on a plane home. The embassy was naive in believing the police would let this drop. Everything we had witnessed and experienced since the police had dragged us into their country made it virtually certain they would pursue this to the bitter end. It didn't matter that we hadn't done anything wrong or broken any laws. What mattered was their standing and credibility in the eyes of the nation and the world.

The consulate was not savvy or sharp enough to see this was always going to happen. From my perspective, officials seemed to sit back and let all the opportunities to apply pressure slip by. The Foreign Office guys back in London should have been in touch with their counterparts in New Delhi before the appeal went in, pushing to get our passports back, and trying to get their fellow countrymen out of this mess. Instead, our nightmare continued.

When Q Branch lodged the appeal, we were half-expecting a suitable reaction from our embassy. You would have thought that officials would have been shocked, embarrassed, or even sorry for messing things up. They had badly misjudged the response of the Indian police, and now they looked foolish. But we didn't get an apology. The government never said sorry. We just got a bland, "Well, we didn't think it would happen."

I, for one, couldn't let this go. I wasn't going to sit around helplessly and allow this happen to me. I decided to act on my own initiative. I would go and see Madam Q Branch, as I called her – the boss, the woman in charge, the only one who could call off the dogs – and stop her department from pursuing this appeal.

I found out I could get a chit in lieu of a passport. I got a few photos printed and brought legal paperwork with me, as well as the letters from my lawyers, and I went down to police HQ, demanding to see the woman in charge. Officers on duty were more than a little startled to see me standing there. They tried to persuade me to leave, but I was determined, and I told them no. I insisted I wanted to see the boss lady.

As usual, they made me wait. I was there for hours, but I refused to give up. When Madam Q Branch emerged and saw me, it was a relief. She immediately leaned towards one of her underlings and said something in Tamil. I didn't speak the language, but I could tell the thrust of what she was saying by her body language and the expression on her face. She was telling her assistant to interrupt her in a few minutes, so she could get out of our meeting before it became awkward. In the end, that was exactly what happened.

Madam Q Branch was a small woman with dark, shoulder-length hair. She wore glasses and civilian clothes, like the rest of CID, so she would either be dressed in a skirt, trousers or, sometimes, a sari. No doubt, she had a family somewhere but that didn't make her care about mine. Mostly, she liked to pretend that our situation was nothing to do with her.

I don't know what she was expecting, but I didn't go down there to have a shouting match. I didn't like the woman, but I couldn't see the point in creating a confrontation. That would have got me nowhere. In fact, I was hoping to appeal to her better nature, if she had one. Under the circumstances, I was very polite. I spelt out the anguish that had been caused to my family because of the actions of the coastguard and the police. I explained that my mother was critically ill, and I wanted to go home so I could be with her. I reminded her that the case had been quashed by the High Court, and rightly so, because we had done nothing wrong. I told her, "We protect Indian sailors."

It was always going to be a long shot, but I had to try. Perhaps deep down, I hoped that by explaining my situation, she might start to see us as real people with homes and loved ones that we were missing and who were missing us. If that was the case, I was about to be disappointed. None of my words meant anything. She listened to me, heard me out, then said, "We will let the courts decide." It was as if none of this was anything to do with her. She was washing her hands of our plight.

I couldn't leave it at that. I told her. "You can end this now. It's up to you if you decide to appeal the verdict. You don't have to do that."

I got a dead-eyed look from her as she repeated her meaningless words. "We will let the courts decide."

It was clear that she didn't care about me or any of the other guys. My words about my critically ill mother barely registered, and she didn't give a damn about our role protecting Indian sailors. None of that mattered. She just wanted to see us convicted and sent to prison for years, simply to prove a point.

If you are wondering why I refer to the woman in charge as "Madam Q Branch", that's how I knew her as back then and how I see her now. Her real name was hard to pronounce, let alone spell, and her behaviour towards us was so inflexible that it just seemed appropriate to give her a bureaucratic label instead of a name. I will always think of her as Madam Q Branch, the cruel head of an evil administration.

It was another long year before our case was finally heard by the Indian Supreme Court. In that time, there were no charges against the men, or any bail conditions imposed. We were technically free but, because we couldn't return home, it felt like something very far from freedom.

In July 2015, in what was to be the latest in a long line of cruel blows, the justices overturned the ruling of the High Court, reinstated the charges and insisted we go to trial. That meant waiting for another long, painful and arduous six months until our case would receive its final verdict.

CHAPTER 25

ESCAPE!

There were a few times when I thought I couldn't go on any longer because there were too many obstacles ahead. That's when I felt like giving up. When I hit absolute rock bottom all I could think was, how can I end this nightmare?

Of course, there was one obvious way out but, no matter how low I felt, I never seriously contemplated killing myself. Suicide was never an option. Even if it had played on my mind, I couldn't imagine going through with the act because of the effect it would have had on my family.

Still, with no way out, I started to feel desperate. I felt particularly bad that I couldn't be there with my mam as she battled ill-health. It was terrible being so far away from her and feeling so completely helpless.

All the stress and worry began to turn me into a different person. I was on my own for a lot of the time. I started to become selfish in my thinking and only consider my own ordeal. For a while, my situation seemed so bad, I felt I didn't have the capacity to worry about the other lads. I needed out and it had to be fast. I was prepared to do whatever it took to get away from Chennai and return home. That was all I cared about for a while, and it was then that I first seriously began to consider escape.

The idea started to form in my mind more seriously after I made contact with a former member of the Parachute Regiment in Mumbai. He was living there because he was married to an Indian girl. This was a guy I had known from my time in 1 Para, so I knew I could trust him. He listened patiently when I told him all we had been through, and he couldn't believe the magnitude of the injustice. By the summer of 2015, we had been arrested, put in prison on remand for months, had our bail granted, and revoked, then granted again. Our charges had been levelled, thrown out, and appealed, then reinstated, and now, more than two years after we had first been dragged to India by the coastguard, we were finally facing trial and a very uncertain future. The stress of all that had been unbelievable, and I was finally at the end of my tether. I was close to cracking, in fact.

My old Para mate had about as much faith in the Indian judicial system as I had, and he offered to help. I won't tell you his name because he is still out there, and I don't want him to get into any trouble. He said he could put me in contact with people who could sell me a fake visa. My new documents would make it appear as if I were a tourist on holiday in India. These people could then help me to get over the border and away. It all sounded so simple and, in my frame of mind at that time, it started to sound like a very tempting solution.

He reckoned if I possessed a fake visa, I could just brazen it out by walking into an airport and catching a flight out of the country.

I wasn't so sure. It seemed to me it would be harder to pass through security at an airport, especially as I didn't have my passport. He suggested an alternative. He said it might be easier to slip some money to a fisherman and take a boat out of India instead. If I could get hold of a couple of grand somehow, and pay the right guy, I could slip quietly out of port one night. He reckoned a fishing boat could take me 250 miles to Sri Lanka. I would be free.

All of a sudden, I started to believe this was not only the best solution for me, but perhaps the only way out. The longer we worked it through, the more I started to think that this plan was possible and might actually happen. At one point I convinced myself that I was seriously going to go for it.

That's not to say I didn't have my doubts. How would I know who I could trust? What if I chose the wrong guy on the wrong boat? It was a big risk, knowing he could take my money then disappear, or shop me to the police, with all the extra trouble that would bring. The police had made enough of a fuss about our supposed criminality already. I could only imagine the shit I'd be in if I was caught trying to flee the country illegally.

I started to waver on the idea of escaping by boat – and my other options didn't look so great either. They would involve me heading inland and travelling cross-country. In theory that might have been the safest option. I could travel by foot, by bus, train or car... but whichever way I tried it, this would be one hell of a journey. And I would still have the same problems with my documents. They would have to stand up to official scrutiny, and the pressure would surely rise once the authorities launched a high-profile manhunt.

India was a very big country. It was hard to get my head around. The entire surface area of the UK could fit into India 13 times. The distances involved in moving from place to place were crazy too. Tamil Nadu covered nearly 20,000 square miles and was only the 11th biggest state in India. Just travelling from Chennai to Tuticorin would take nine hours. That was like driving from London to Inverness. The idea that I could move easily across this vast country without being stopped and re-arrested seemed impossible.

India's geographical position didn't help. It bordered Pakistan and China, neither of which I fancied visiting, particularly as a fugitive. Chennai to Pakistan was 1,300 miles and Chennai to China 1,500. Even if I could manage to cover so much ground and cross that border, what would happen to me then? What would they do with me?

I suspected China, in particular, wouldn't be too chuffed to have a former member of the British armed forces arrive in the country illegally. At the very least, both China and Pakistan would view me as an uninvited foreigner in their land. Worse, as an ex-military man, they could very likely view me as a spy. I couldn't imagine any scenario where my discovery in a potentially hostile foreign country could possibly end well. I might have ended up swapping one horrendous foreign prison for another. Although I was in a bad state, it was perfectly possible that things could still get a lot worse for me. A charge of spying would be a lot more serious than the trumped-up weapons offences I presently faced.

I gave it a hell of a lot of thought but, in the end, I realised that none of this was very practical. More importantly, I had also begun to think more clearly and less selfishly about my situation. For the sake of argument, imagine if I had managed to use all my training to escape and evade the police and leave the country. Imagine also I somehow managed to get all the way home to Ashington. What then?

I would be creating a nightmare for the guys I left behind. I'd be dropping them all right in the shit.

I knew how the Indian authorities would react if I fled the country. They would reason I must have been guilty all along and, by extension, the other lads were guilty too. That's what they would have claimed in court, and my crewmates would pay the price for my selfishness. I didn't want to mess things up for the men I left behind. They would be tarnished by my apparent guilt and put in worse peril as a result.

As soon as I realised that likely outcome, I stopped thinking so narrowly and gave up on the whole idea. I saw it for what it was: a fanciful notion that was purely self-centred because I was under extreme pressure. I put all thoughts of escape out of my mind and resolved to stay and do the right thing. I wasn't going anywhere. Whatever happened next, we would all stand and fall together.

CHAPTER 26

FACING THE MUSIC

People might think that this long spell in India wasn't so bad, and certainly not as bad as prison. That was true, of course, but my life was never in my own hands. I was living with the possibility of a long jail sentence hanging over me the whole time. For 18 months, I was in limbo, not a criminal or a prisoner, but not free or innocent either. Whenever I thought about the prospect of returning to prison, it only confirmed my determination never to go back there.

In the run up to the trial, we still had hope that an Indian court would finally show some common sense. It seemed so obvious that the evidence was in our favour, we continued to believe that some court at some time would eventually acknowledge the obvious truth.

Once the trial was finally underway in late 2015, the lawyers began to suggest it was going well, and there was a good chance that the charges would be thrown out again. This was a rare piece of welcome news.

I didn't go to court every day. We weren't forced to attend, mainly because there were so many of us, and the Indians didn't want 35 burly blokes gathered at the back of the courtroom. I only travelled when I was told I had to go. The journey to Tuticorin District Principal Sessions Court, in the south of India, took 10 hours from Chennai, and most of the time I learned absolutely nothing by being there. The whole trial was conducted in Tamil, and we had no-one to translate the proceedings and evidence for us, so we didn't understand a word. The court would send us transcripts afterwards, but there was no point trying to follow our trial as it happened. That was a waste of time. We just had to trust in the lawyers and the evidence and hope for the best.

I had every faith in Ray and Paul, who worked hard to make sure our lawyers had all the documents they needed. They explained our situation in detail to the legal team for the trial that had been arranged by ITF Seafarers, a charitable maritime trust. The team was led by Mr Muthusamy from Anand, Samy & Dhruva. The lads knew what they were doing. In fact, without Ray, Mr Muthusamy would have been lost. I want to thank him for that. He basically built our defence. He organised all the paperwork that covered the weapons charges, and that was no mean feat.

The lawyers kept us posted when anything important happened, and they continued to be optimistic all the way through the trial. They knew the coastguard and the police were lying. Their testimony, which was vague and contradictory, lacked facts and relevant evidence. They were pretty sure the judge – who was sitting without a jury – would be able to see right through it too, although, to me, he always looked like he didn't care either way.

The trial started in September 2015 and eventually finished the following January. It took them more than four months to hear a simple matter involving some weapons and the navigational positioning of our ship. That's how shambolic the courts were.

The prosecution struggled to make a convincing argument that we were trespassing in Indian waters. It didn't help their case when they showed themselves incapable of proving exactly where we were when the coastguard boarded the Seaman Guard Ohio. At one point a large map was unfolded in court so they could highlight our exact position for the judge. They couldn't do it. Their navigational equipment wasn't working at the time, and they tried to bullshit the judge that we were much closer to India than we actually were. They did this by starting their measurements, not from the mainland, but from an uninhabited island 12 nautical miles offshore that was not even a recognised part of the Indian coast. They were using an outcrop far out to sea where nobody lived as the basis of their case for our intrusion into territorial waters.

The whole issue of our navigational position was ridiculous anyway. We never lied about our position, but we made the strong case that we were covered under maritime law. We had moved closer inland during adverse weather conditions, and we had absolutely no intention of going into an Indian port, at least not until we were forced there by the coastguard.

In any case, none of this had anything to do with me, any of the Chennai Six, or the Estonian lads. We weren't in charge of the ship, or its navigational position. We were just crew. If you wanted to be harsh, you could have held the captain or his officers accountable for those decisions, but we were just passengers. It had nowt to do with us.

The weapons charges affected us more directly and, to prove the case against us, the prosecution brought in a so-called ballistics expert. He said we had illegal weapons on board, but our ballistics expert immediately destroyed his argument. The key point was the claim that we were carrying automatic weapons, which were illegal aboard ships conducting anti-piracy operations.

Our guy brought one of the G3s into the court and demonstrated what they could and couldn't do. He asked the prosecution if they had tested any of the weapons on fully automatic mode, and they admitted they had only fired two rounds, which was ridiculous. To test a gun properly and fully understand its capabilities, they should have fired off a whole magazine at the very least.

It didn't help that the police were living in the dark ages when it came to weapons. Their police carried guns that looked as if they dated back to the 1900s. Some of them carried first world war era rifles. A few of the better equipped officers carried auto or semi-automatic weapons, but they were in awe of the Heckler & Koch G3. It was designed to be a weapon of war. Like the famous Kalashnikov AK47, the G3 could be used as a machine gun but, with a change of setting, it could fire a single shot at a time. The weapons we used had parts removed, which meant they couldn't be fired on automatic. Our ballistics guy demonstrated that fact for the judge. Those parts could not be retro-fitted to the G3s. It was physically impossible. The guns had been welded to ensure that could never happen. There was no way to fire them on fully auto. He proved this in court. We thought that would be enough, surely.

Our expert also showed that the weapons had certificates and all their necessary documentation in place. Everything was in order and as it should be. The judge listened and replied, "Duly noted."

We genuinely believed he had taken this crucial evidence on board and began to hope for a favourable outcome.

We even started to wonder if the whole case might be done by Christmas 2015. Perhaps we could be home with our families for a special festive celebration. But that hope faded as the weeks dragged by. The judge decided against bringing in the verdict at the end of the case but, instead, he ordered a two-week interlude over Christmas and the New Year, with the big decision date set for 10 January 2016. We could, and should, have been home for Christmas, but the Indian courts were going to string this out for as long as possible, we could tell. However, we went off for the festive break clinging to the positive reports from our lawyers. Our case had been well set out, and it was clearly much stronger than the prosecution case. We could only hope that would be enough.

CHAPTER 27

THE VERDICT

I spent Christmas and the New Year with Monalisa in Bangalore, about 200 miles inland from Chennai. It was cooler there, and a lot more civilised. On Christmas Day, I video-called my family, so I could at least get to see and talk to them even if it was from the other side of the world. Then I went to a hotel for Christmas lunch. I couldn't relax. I had the verdict hanging over me the whole time, but we were all cautiously optimistic, despite everything that a corrupt and incompetent system had thrown at us.

I reminded myself that our lawyers had told us it was all looking very positive, and I had every reason to believe I would be back in Ashington by the end of January. We felt we had a very strong case. It had been presented well by our lawyers, and the police case against us had been picked apart and exposed as lies. There was nothing more that could have been done on our behalf in court. Even though we knew we were in the lion's den, we hoped the judge might finally recognise this case for what it was – a fabrication.

But I also knew that Tamil Nadu was a law unto itself. The vast south-eastern state was considered primitive even by fellow Indians, who tended to look down on the place. Even after 70 years of independence, I felt there was a very strong anti-British sentiment festering in that part of India. While I appreciated the native population had suffered greatly during the era of the British Empire, it was a very long time ago and it had nothing to do with me. However, my instincts told me a lingering resentment was a major factor in the way we were being treated. Why else would they ignore facts and evidence and place us in a position where we were facing prison on trumped-up charges?

As the day of the verdict drew nearer, I went over the case again and again in my mind. I tried to see our case as the judge might see it and then tried to predict the outcome from that perspective. I knew we had made a strong argument and we had done nothing wrong. Our lawyers were confident the evidence against us had been firmly and thoroughly discredited, and they had concluded we would be acquitted. But I had the bitter experience of false hope in the past, and I hadn't fully changed my opinion that we were far from in the clear.

I was convinced the police and the courts were going to stitch us up, and I made sure I was vocal about it. I was convinced I knew where this was going. I had repeatedly told the Foreign Office guys, "If we don't get this all resolved before it goes to trial, they will find us guilty of something, and we will definitely go to prison."

For some reason, representatives of Her Majesty's Government didn't see it that way. They looked at the evidence the same way our lawyers had done and concluded the authorities had nothing on us. They were convinced that, because we hadn't done anything wrong and we were clearly innocent, everything would work out fine. I told them the facts and the evidence didn't matter. That wasn't the point of this trial. We were up against an entire state here, and the guardians of that state would do whatever they liked to make it work. If they wanted to send us down, then that's what would happen. But no-one heeded my warning. No-one was listening.

On the last day in court on 11 January 2016, we knew a decision on our fate was moments away. We heard the judge's assistant shout something. It sounded as if it might be the verdict but, of course, he spoke in Tamil. Court officials didn't bother to translate even this vital moment into English for us. We had to wait for someone to let us know what had been said. We would be the last to know the decision that would determine the course of our lives. There was no clue in the judge's expression. He had such a poker face on him.

The two Tamil girls from the embassy, Sharon and Manisha, heard the verdict, and one of them left the courtroom straight away to phone the Deputy High Commissioner. The other just sat there in shock and didn't say a word. We were still left hanging. Only when the police officers filed in did we get a strong signal about how it had gone. We were hardly going to start a riot if the ruling had gone in our favour, were we? This looked really bad now. I was worried. I knew the maximum prison sentence for possession of illegal firearms was seven years. If we had been found guilty, what would the judge give us? When the lawyer came over to speak to Billy, Paul and Ray, I was off to the side of them and straining to hear what was being said. Then I heard the conversation and my worst fears were confirmed.

Guilty.

Five years.

Even though I had always suspected they would find us guilty in the end, I'd allowed myself to be swayed by our optimistic lawyers and a deep-down belief that, even in a place like India, justice might just be possible. But to hear out loud, confirmed as fact, this cruel verdict, that was a huge and devastating blow. Five years! Jesus. None of us expected that. Initially, shock was the only thing I could feel. How could this be? It should have been over. We should have been on our way home. Our lawyers had proved the prosecution case was a pack of lies. How could we have lost a court case when the evidence against us had been systematically picked apart and exposed? How could the judge turn justice on its head and send us to prison when he could see we were innocent? It was a truly gut-wrenching and shattering moment.

We should have known better. Like I said, I knew in my heart of hearts it was never going to go our way. The judge had listened to the evidence presented on our behalf, then deliberately ignored it. How else could he have delivered a guilty verdict resulting in a five-year sentence?

We shouldn't have been surprised. We had spoken to enough Indians who told us how it was with their legal system. They told us we would have to bribe our way out of prison and off the hook. They told us to pay off the police and we would probably be all right. The whole system was owned by the police. If they decided that we were guilty then we were guilty. It might sound dramatic, but that was the way it was. I never saw anything the whole time I was in India to make me change my mind.

As shocked as we were by the outcome, we quickly understood it was likely to be a very long while before we would be getting out of this nightmare and going home. We were heading back to prison, and there was nothing we could do about it.

Before we left the courtroom, there was time for one last bizarre episode. We were ordered to get our conviction paperwork personally from the judge, and we were told we could have a final word with him. What the hell use would that be after the verdict? It was ridiculous. When I collected my paperwork, I looked the judge in the eye and told him, "You've made a big, big mistake." He wasn't the least bit interested and didn't bat an eyelid. He just didn't care at all.

Madam Q Branch scarpered straight away. She'd done her job and high-tailed it out of there as soon as she heard the verdict. Did she feel remorse? I don't think so, or she wouldn't have pushed for our prosecution in the first place. She could have intervened to ensure it never went to trial at all, like I asked her to. It would have just ended.

When we left the courtroom, the Indian press met us outside, snapping away at us with their cameras as we piled onto the prison bus. A BBC news crew was waiting too, and reporters asked us for a reaction to the verdict and our five-year sentence. When I found myself in front of a TV camera, I had an urgent message to deliver to the prime minister, David Cameron. I begged him to do everything he could to get his countrymen released and end this nightmare.

The embassy was busy trying to sort out practical matters now we were certain to be heading to prison. We had all been staying in different hotels and hostels, and we needed help to pack up all our kit and have it sent somewhere for safekeeping. At the same time, we were urging consulate officials to tell the Foreign Office exactly what was going on and put pressure on government to do something to help us.

Before we were dragged away, I had just enough time to make the phone call I dreaded the most. The call home to tell Lisa. When she picked up, I told her what had happened, and I said, "Lisa, you are going to need to get to mam's now, and you'll have to tell her for me."

I rang my dad and told him, "It's not good news. They sentenced us to five years." He couldn't believe it.

"You are fucking joking, aren't you?" he said. He doesn't show much emotion my dad. The only other time I recall him losing his cool was when I went to Afghanistan, not long after some poor blokes had been blown up out there. He was worried about me then, but now he was just plain furious.

Lisa was so upset she told me she couldn't bring herself to tell mam. I would have to do that. She put me on speakerphone. I said, "Mam, I've been sentenced to five years." That's when a horrible scream came down the phone. It's a scream I never want to hear again. If she had actually seen me dead, she couldn't have made a more anguished noise.

To mam, her baby boy was innocent, and now he had been locked up in a foreign country at the other end of the world for five long years. It was horrible. Right then, I felt like my heart had been ripped out.

CHAPTER 28

WE WILL ANNIHILATE YOU

I was so angry, frustrated and desperate after the verdict I just wanted to unleash hell, but what was that going to achieve? Even in the depths of my despair, I knew the answer to that. Nothing.

Punching a guard, starting a riot, ripping the seats out of the bus? None of that was going to get me anywhere, except into even bigger trouble. I was absolutely raging but, somehow, I managed to keep myself from going completely crazy. I kept my emotions under control.

After the five-year sentence was handed down, the guards drove us away, but we didn't go straight to prison. First, they took us all to the hospital. I honestly believe we were sent there because the authorities hadn't worked out what to do with us yet. They were so pathetically disorganised, they needed time to work out the best place to put us. At first, it looked like we might even have to spend the next five years in Palayamkottai Central prison in Tirunelveli. That was the prison we were taken to when we were first arrested almost three years earlier, and we heard we might be going back. No way would we all survive. That was the simple truth. The place was a hell-hole. Even three days there felt like a lifetime. How could we last five years?

I don't how the Indian crew members survived in Palayamkottai. They were separated from us and left there, supposedly for protection in case they were targeted because of their association with us. But that also meant they were living in the worst possible conditions. I dreaded the idea of returning.

We sat in that hospital for 90 minutes while the police decided what to do with us. It was a long, uncertain wait, and I spent the time coming to terms with the fact that the news about our destination might actually prove worse than the verdict. Eventually, they called us back onto the bus, and we found out we had a 14-hour drive north ahead of us. We weren't going to Palayamkottai. They were taking us back to prison in Chennai. This was almost a relief at the time, compared to the alternative.

When we were on remand in Chennai, we were placed in Puzhal Central Prison 2, where we stayed for months until we were granted bail. Now we had been convicted of a crime, we were sent to Puzhal Central prison 1, which was part of the same site, but contained more hardened criminals. These were the guys who had been found guilty of major crimes, and some of them were serving very long sentences for murder or rape, so they didn't give a shit about anything.

As we were led into the prison, we were all wondering what impact these developments were having back in the UK. What was the consulate in Chennai doing about the sentence? What were they thinking in the embassy in New Delhi? We were told that the UK government was shocked by the decision of the court. That might have been true, but the politicians had let this farce go on for years without intervening, so they couldn't have cared all that much. None of that mattered to any of us anyway. We were all back in prison together and, somehow, we had to find a way to get through this.

With 23 men all crammed together in one big cell, all of us digesting a crushing verdict, there were tensions and arguments. Proper fist fights broke out. It didn't help that there were Ukrainians, Estonians and Russian/Estonians mixed together, and some did not get on at all.

Luckily, after a few weeks, the prison guards gave us another cell, so five of us Brits, Paul, Billy, John, Ray and I, left the main cell and went downstairs into that one. With five in a room, our living situation had improved, but it was still cramped, and people still got irate every now and then. That was inevitable when a bunch of blokes had to share a confined space together in extreme conditions.

After years in the Paras, I'd slept rough outdoors on enough occasions to be able to bed down virtually anywhere for the night. But the hard floor took its toll. We eventually told our jailers, "You can't expect us to sleep on concrete for five years." For once they listened and grudgingly allowed us to cadge old, thin mattresses from the prison hospital. It wasn't exactly luxury, but I was raised off the ground, so I was certainly not complaining. After that, I went to the prison shop where they made uniforms, resulting in loads of scraps of material left over. I gave a guy there a couple of packs of Bidis and asked him to use those scraps to make me a small pillow. That made my nights a little more comfortable.

At least the kitchen was across the road from our compound and not a mile away like before. The walk there was much better than when we were on remand, running the gauntlet, taking abuse, and having missiles lobbed at us when we went for water or food.

There were other improvements too compared to life in the first prison. I clung to each one so I could tell myself that life here could be made more bearable. It wasn't as overcrowded as the remand prison. We received food parcels, and we could buy food as well. There was a shop, and the prison ran a card system that allowed us to use some of our own money. We were even permitted to spend more than the Indian inmates.

One of the guys managed to buy a pipe with a shower head. We attached it to the water supply, so we could rig up a shower of sorts, which saved us having to wash in a bucket. It was an improvised solution that meant a lot at the time. We were forever trying to make up for losing the comforts we took for granted when we were back home.

Maybe it is something deep within me, or simply the training I received when I was in the Paras, but I believed that I had to make the situation work, however difficult the circumstances. It helped that I was reminded that there were always people worse off than myself. Take my cellmate Paul Towers, a man who commanded my greatest respect. He was 23 years older than me and was like a father figure while I was in prison. We helped each other along as we battled to keep our spirits up. Every day was tough, but I have to admit I had it much easier than Paul. I had no wife or kids waiting for me at home, no mortgage to worry about or dependants to provide for. Paul had all those things, and he was trapped out there with me and the rest of the lads. I realised that the only thing I really had to worry about was me and the struggle to find the inner strength to make it through to the other side.

We were all desperate to get home as soon as possible, but I took the view from the outset that there was no point in bitching, moaning and crying because it wouldn't make any difference. I was determined to adopt a military mental attitude. I wanted to show resilience and never look down in the dumps no matter how I felt.

I told myself that if I had to do five years, I would *do* five years, then walk out of there with my head held high. They could put me in a cell, but I was going to show these people that they would never break my spirit or dent my pride. I wanted every guard in that prison to see me and think that I looked OK, even when I was suffering. I knew they would expect me to sink into a terrible state, but I didn't want to give them the satisfaction of seeing that misery etched on my face. I also knew that my sister would be doing everything in her power to push and push to get me released. I could not let down my family, the thousands of people who supported us, or my regiment. And I would definitely not let myself down. I refused to do that.

I often wondered if my positive attitude was forged by my time in the Paras, or if I always thought that way. I think it was a bit of both. I had always been mentally strong. That was how I won a place in the regiment in the first place. As an 18-year-old, I had to cope with a Parachute Regiment sergeant major screaming at me. Because he was local, I had more to prove than most. That increased the pressure, but also made me more determined to succeed. My type of mentality thrived in the Paras. I kept a positive, robust attitude during selection, and I always knew that I could call on those qualities when I faced life's toughest tests. When the biggest test arrived, spanning over four years in India, that resilience was essential. Besides, I had no option. I couldn't pick up the phone and ask to come home. I had no-one. I knew I had to show determination and pride, and never, ever give in.

I had worked so hard to become a Para. It was tattooed on my arm and buried deep in my heart. As a former member, I always knew I was always representing the Parachute Regiment while I was out in India, and I used that thought to spur me on. It would have been so easy to give up. I wanted to, more than once, and I could have thrown it all away, but I had made it this far. I called on my strength and experience and, at that moment, something ignited in me. I told myself, "Get a grip and give your head a wobble, remember what is on your right shoulder and drive to the finish."

* * *

After prisoners had served some prison time in Chennai, they were allowed to apply to go home. They could obtain weekend leave passes and could even request home visits lasting for a month. Can you imagine the comments in the UK if a killer or child rapist was released back into the community for weeks at a time? There would be outrage. But not here. You would see these guys walking out of the jail, all suited and booted, smiling and smelling of aftershave.

Some of the Indian prisoners never wanted to leave. We were in a very poor country and these people were better off in the jail where they would be fed and housed. A future outside the prison walls didn't guarantee even those meagre comforts.

I would have chewed off my right leg for a chance to go home for a few days. But none of us believed for one moment the authorities would let us out. They gave permission to their own people and were supposed to spread the invitation to foreigners as well, but we recognised there was no chance of that happening.

Then one day, embassy officials approached us and said there might be a way out of India. This would involve us going home before our sentence was complete. Of course, we wanted to hear more. Apparently, we could apply for a prison transfer to the UK and finish our sentence in a British prison. Conditions would have been a lot better back home for sure, and we would have been out of India forever – but there was a catch. And it was a big one. To apply for this scheme, we would have to admit our guilt. There was no way I was ever going to do that. I had done nothing wrong, and there was no incentive on the table that was going to make me say otherwise. When the embassy officials brought the paperwork to check if we were interested, I told them to take it away. I said I'd rather do five years and keep my head held high than admit guilt for something I hadn't done just because I couldn't hack prison life in India.

My decision wasn't just about keeping my good name. I had to think about the future. If I admitted guilt, I would have a permanent criminal record. I would never be able to work legitimately anywhere again, in the UK or abroad.

I also reminded the rest of the lads, "You don't think they'll just put us in an open prison, do you? These are offences involving guns, which means you will be inside a proper British prison with hardened criminals who are probably a lot tougher than the so-called hard men over here. Forget these wannabe gangsters, there's a good chance you'd get stabbed for real in there."

It wasn't easy to turn our backs on the one real possibility of getting out of Indian jail before five years of our lives had been used up – but it was the right thing to do. I had no doubt about that. I didn't know what was going to happen to us in future, but I did understand that we had to stay strong and keep our heads above water. We were all suffering, but we could not let the Indian authorities come out on top. As much as anything, this was a mental battle, and we had to be the victors.

If I hadn't been a Para and undergone all that training, everything about my ordeal would have been a whole lot harder. But even my training had its limits. After a while, when the days became weeks, and the weeks became months, and the months turned into a year, it became truly difficult, and there still seemed to be no end in sight. I began to struggle mentally. Even in extreme conditions, I had an ability to cope with anything thrown at me, but I realised that my normal reserves of strength were not going to be enough to get me through. I had to accept that I didn't have the regiment watching my back any more. I was on my own. I can remember telling myself, "Fuck this Para business. You are going to have to take this to the next level if you want to survive here. You have to get through all of it by yourself. It's the only way."

I made a conscious decision to take every day as it came and just focus on getting through each one. I decided to put my personal struggles out of my mind and not dwell on my situation too much. I told myself to get my head down and get on with it.

Of course, refusing to acknowledge the difficulties had a downside. I was storing up trouble. When this chapter of my life was finally over and done with, I recognised that the trauma could all come flooding back, hitting me harder. There was a real danger of a proper meltdown. I'd heard enough cases of post-traumatic stress disorder when I was out in Afghanistan and Iraq to understand the risks. Even so, I had to stick to my strategy, at least while I was trapped here. It was a mental thing. I could not afford to dwell on the negative for too long while I was in prison. It was the only way to survive without driving myself crazy.

Besides, I was facing enough physical risks to keep my mind occupied. There were all sorts of "characters" in the prison with us. These were people I would have seriously avoided in civilian life. Now we were all banged up together, and we had to constantly watch our backs. There was this one guy we all called Slasher. His whole body was covered in scars, but that wasn't how he had earned his nickname. This fella had somehow managed to hollow out a small section of the inside of his cheek where he could hide a razor blade. He used to make a point of removing the blade with his tongue to show everyone. How he managed that trick without slicing off his tongue I'll never know, but he thought he was rock-hard and liked to show this razor to send a message. He was saying, "Come near me and I'll slice you." When he performed his little trick near us, we used to tell him to wind his neck in. While he was an idiot and an attention seeker, he was also a convicted murderer, and we couldn't afford to forget what he could do to us. Slasher was finally released after 15 years or so, and he's probably out there somewhere today on the streets of Chennai. Probably still got that bloody razor blade in his mouth too.

In prison, my enemy's enemy was my friend, so sometimes we ended up cautiously buddying up with people on that basis. But we were always aware of the dangers. We kept everyone at arm's length. We met some Nigerian lads who were all drug dealers, but we still played football and volleyball with them. They were in prison for dealing heroin but, in that prison, they were harmless by comparison. Once they got to know us, they said they wanted to stay in touch after their sentences were complete, and they gave us their phone numbers and email addresses. I didn't fancy that to be honest. I was in enough trouble as it was without staying pally with a bunch of heroin dealers once I got out of jail.

Not all the Indians hated us. Some of them realised they could make a bit of money from an association with the westerners. One guy used to do our ironing and smuggle in lighters so we could smoke. It was a weird system in prison when it came to cigarettes. The authorities would let you buy Indian cigs, Bidis, and we were allowed to smoke them, but they wouldn't let us have matches. Lighters were considered contraband, and we weren't allowed to bring them in openly, but if we managed to get hold of one and we were spotted by the guards, they wouldn't take it off us. I took up smoking in prison then weaned myself off again when I came out. A pack of Bidis in India cost around 40p, but back home it was £9.50 a pack. There was no way I was paying that. Before, when I was out on bail, I'd see Indian guys buying cigarettes in ones and twos and I couldn't understand why. Then I noticed they were buying chewing gum as well, and I figured it out. These Indians were all secret smokers. They would have a crafty fag or two then chew the gum on the way home to mask the smell.

Despite some of the inmates tolerating us, the prison was still a hostile place. We were seen as the enemy by most of the Indians just because we were different. I was always alive to the possibility of violence flaring at any moment and, to be honest, there were times when I would have welcomed a break in the tension. The way I felt, it would have been a release to take out my frustrations on someone else. Most of the time I was able to keep this urge in check. That was most of the time – but not always. Everyone had their breaking point, and I was about to reach mine.

I was told to report to the prison doctor, and I wasn't happy. I didn't like the bloke. He was a horrible bastard who used to shout at us all the time. I didn't take kindly to that. I'd be in the army, and I'd been shouted at by the best. This guy didn't remotely have the standing of a sergeant in the Paras. He hadn't earned my respect. This fella was unbelievable, and he always had the arse. I turned up that day, and he started shouting at me because I didn't have a chit, the signed permission slip he was after. He was shouting and demanding to know where it was, and I started shouting back that I was only there because he was the one who had asked me to attend.

I tried to explain myself, but he kept on shouting and pushing me and pushing me until something inside me finally snapped. I had been keeping my emotions in check for so long, but this was too much. I lost my temper visibly and shouted him down. He must have felt threatened, and that didn't work out so well for me because other prisoners saw the confrontation and how I was loading on this guy. They knew they'd get Brownie points for sticking up for the doctor, particularly if they appeared to be protecting him from attack. They surrounded me, then manhandled and threatened me. It looked like the stand-off was going to escalate and properly kick off. All the months of frustration and anger were boiling up inside me, and I just lost it. I left – but I told them I'd be back.

I'd had enough. I found a metal pipe and was heading back to the hospital when a few of the other guys stopped me. They talked me down and convinced me to dump my weapon. Finally, we agreed we would all go together to confront this mob of angry prisoners who had been threatening to sort me out.

I told the doctor I was sorry for shouting, and I was happy to start the appointment again, but if anyone was thinking of trying anything stupid, I had my guys to back me up this time. One of the Indian inmates, a supposed gangster, decided to test our resolve. He wanted to start something there and then, but when he made his move, my mate smashed a headbutt into him. There was a massive crack, and he just crumpled. He went down hard, hit the floor and stayed there.

All hell broke loose. There were fights brewing all around me. Punches were thrown, prisoners were grappling with each other, and a number of bodies hit the ground. In the middle of it all, someone tried to lamp me with a crutch, so I grabbed it and yanked it away. Then another Indian bloke punched me. It was complete pandemonium all around, with bodies being thrown about and fists flying. At the height of this, I stupidly turned my back on a guy as he picked up a metal chair to use as a weapon against me. It was as if I had forgotten all my army training for a second, and a second was all it took. It was a stupid thing to do.

As I turned back round, he was about to land his hefty blow. Just before it landed, one of the prison guards grabbed the chair and disarmed him. Without that intervention I'd have been seriously injured. Later, I shook the guard by the hand and thanked him. There was no time for gratitude now, though. We were two groups facing off one against another, and we were ready and able to cause serious injury if the violence started again. We were outnumbered big style, but some of our guys were massive.

But the arrival of that guard seemed to signal the end of the stand-off. I told the Indian inmates, "Keep away from us from now on and there will be no dramas, but if you try and come at us again, we will annihilate you."

That did the trick. They must have looked at this group of big blokes, and the damage we had caused and, suddenly, they weren't so keen on a scrap. They must have got the message because we never had any more trouble after that, at least not from the inmates.

However, the incident wasn't over. We were hauled before Madam Superintendent Rukmani Priyadarshi, and it looked like we were in the shit, particularly when we learned that prison guards – who weren't even in the room – had written fake reports that firmly attached the blame to us. The superintendent was a short, slightly plump woman with dark hair, and she wore the usual beige prison uniform. She was also very well spoken and clearly educated. Thankfully, the superintendent was wise to the prison guards' tricks, and she believed our version of events. That didn't get us entirely off the hook. We were still confined to the compound for three months and escorted everywhere to make sure there was no more aggravation.

Ultimately, the confrontation had been worth it. We managed to assert our authority on the prison. Everyone knew we weren't to be messed with, and we should be left well alone. They could see we would stick together when challenged, and we would crack heads. We wouldn't ever be rolled over by the other inmates. From that moment on, the Indians kept their distance.

CHAPTER 29

LISA'S STORY: VISITING HELL

The first time I visited Nick in Chennai, the guards made us wait outside the prison in scorching heat. I had to stand there with heavy bags full of shopping for Nick and the other men.

The prison guards would stand in a semi-circle around me, holding their guns with bayonets fixed, laughing and staring. I could tell they were talking about me, even though I didn't understand a word of what they were saying. There were female guards there, too, from the women's prison in a separate compound. They were no better. They looked me up and down and glared at me as if I was dirt, even though I always made a point of dressing modestly. I usually wore a shawl and a long skirt, so I was covered up and looked respectable. That didn't stop the dirty looks. In response, I would purposely stand there with my head held high and act like I wasn't bothered – I didn't want to give them the satisfaction.

Every visit was the same. I was made to wait outside for between 30 and 90 minutes before being allowed into the prison compound. It always seemed a lot longer in that heat. It was so exhausting and horrendous.

On my first visit, in March 2014, I made a mistake. Nick had been in prison for five months by now. His birthday was two days after I landed in India, so I brought him lots of presents. I thought it might be fun to wrap them for him, and I even made a joke of it, using pretty princess wrapping paper. But, of course, the prison guards wanted to check everything I was bringing into the prison, so they tore off the wrapping paper, killing the fun, and causing even more of a delay.

When I walked in, Nick was standing there wearing a vest and a short sarong that could have been made from old potato sacking. His hair was all over the place and he looked like a wild man who had been stranded on a desert island. He was thin, his skin was clammy, and he smelt really badly of sweat and dirt. None of that mattered to me. I was finally seeing my brother, and it was a very emotional moment for both of us.

First things first, he asked about mam. I gave him the headlines but not the full story so he wouldn't worry about her too much. I still don't know if I that was the right decision. Maybe I built up his hopes, so when he finally saw her again, he was expecting her to be in better shape. But he knew the score. I remember him saying, "Lisa, I know what an aneurysm is and what it does to you."

When I found out how devastated Nick had been because I stopped sending letters, I felt horrible. It was just awful. I had arranged my visit with the best of intentions. I wanted suddenly to appear out there as a big surprise to Nick, and I had no idea he was beginning to think we had forgotten about him. I felt terrible and made sure I never did it again. I came to understand how important it was for the men to have regular contact with their loved ones.

It wasn't just a simple case of trying to hide my surprise visit. It was way more complicated than that. I was absolutely exhausted and had very little time or energy to write letters. I was trying to hold down a very demanding job as well as go back and forwards to the hospital daily. I spent hours on the internet researching, and I was sending emails to reach out to people, asking for help. I convinced myself that my surprise visit would make up for the missing letters, but that fact was, I was simply struggling to keep all the plates spinning, and something had to give.

Whenever I went to see Nick, I always took in stuff from the families of the other lads. Some of them would come down and say hello. That was good, because I could report back to their loved ones that I had seen them, and they were OK. Whoever was visiting from the UK would always play postman. When it was my turn, I would take in print-outs of emails. I would hand them to the men and wait for them to write a reply, which I would scan into my phone, and email. Because I was doing this not just for the British lads but for the Estonians and Ukrainians too, I'd end up with hundreds of bits of paper to scan and send.

To see Nick in such a state was distressing, but I brought family photos out with me and pictures of Cassie, his dog, and that seemed to cheer him up. These small connections with home gave him a massive boost. On my second visit, I could see the difference. His appearance was transformed. He had shaved, properly washed and used some of the toiletries I had brought in for him. The prison had strange rules. Visitors could take in razors but not bottles of water or dental floss. It was mad. A razor blade could do a lot more damage than dental floss.

During that first visit, we managed to talk about happier stories from back home, and we were able to laugh about them together. Sharon, from the consulate, had accompanied me and she started to laugh too. She said, "It's like you two have never been apart." Once we got talking, we managed to blot out our surroundings and forget about the horrendous situation for a while.

My second visit started very badly. It was very different from the first. In fact, it was terrifying. I was on my own this time – there was no-one from the consulate with me – and the prison authorities made me wait for three hours before they let me into the prison. In India, they loved to keep us waiting for no reason other than to show that they could. It was either a power thing or driven by spite.

Instead of being taken to see Nick, I was led into a large waiting room filled with men, women and children, most of them sitting on the floor. I will always remember the heat, the smell and the flies. And the noise was unbelievable. I had to wait there on my own until eventually I became part of a group that was led outside. A terrible stench hit me. I had never smelt anything like it. The overpowering smell of urine burned my eyes and almost made me gag.

The guards took us into a dark, concrete room. The walls were white but filthy, and there were bars on the window. Wire fencing preventing us from going any further. There was a gap of a few metres behind this fence and then another similar fence. Guards trooped in and lined up to fill the gap between the two fences. That was the signal for a lot of Indian prisoners to flood into the space behind the second fence. The visitors all surged forward. They started screaming and shouting through the fence to their loved ones a few metres away. It was complete chaos.

I couldn't believe what I was seeing. I kept thinking, what is going on? I couldn't possibly talk to Nick in that chaos and confusion. But that didn't matter anyway. He wasn't even there, nor were any of the other guys who were imprisoned with him. I didn't know if this was a mistake, or if this had been done to me intentionally. I wanted to tell someone that this wasn't how it was supposed to be on a visit, but there was no-one to complain to. The guards were sandwiched in the gap between the fences, and I had been left alone in a wild throng of visitors all surging forwards in a desperate attempt to speak to their family members.

I had no protection. If someone had wanted to grab me or stab me, there was nothing or no-one to stop them. I was terrified, but my adrenaline kept me going. I didn't feel safe, but I drew some comfort from the fact that the visitors were too busy trying to communicate with the prisoners to turn their attention to me. The noise was horrendous. The visitors were screaming across the gap between the fences, trying to be heard above the din, and the prisoners were screaming back.

I was there for ages. No-one would talk to me. I was lost and confused. I didn't know what to do. Eventually, a guard beckoned towards me. I followed him, and I was taken back to the superintendent's room. Nick and Paul Towers were standing there. I just hugged Nick and burst into tears. I managed to explain what had happened. Nick and Paul were furious. Nick said there was no way I should have been put through that terrifying ordeal.

Like virtually everything bad that happened in India, we were never sure whether this had occurred because the guards were stupid or malicious. Often, they were simply incompetent. At other times, they made our lives difficult just to be cruel or awkward. You never knew which was which. I just knew I had to stay strong for Nick. That was my mantra. If it wasn't for that, I would have broken down.

On another of my visits, I had to walk through a crowd of gawping prisoners. There was a guard behind me, so they didn't accost me, but I still felt their stares all over me. Many of them had probably never seen a white girl in the flesh before, let alone a blonde one with blue eyes.

We stopped and waited by a room. Outside, there were sandshoes and slippers, and in the room were around 20 inmates on their knees. I wasn't sure what they were doing. I wondered if they might have been praying. Then I realised a guard was interrogating them. He was busy writing, and they were responding to him when he spoke. They were supposed to keep their eyes front and their heads bowed, but they kept sneaking glances at me. Every time one of them looked in my direction, the guard would shout at them, but still they looked. I wasn't alone, but I still felt uneasy.

To be honest, I felt more inhibited by the guards than the prisoners. The first day that I went in on my own, I was searched. I wasn't bothered because I knew that was the routine, even in British prisons. And the search was to be carried out by a woman, so I didn't think anything of it. Not until she patted me down and her hand went inside my clothing. Then she carried on and put her fingers right inside my bra. I thought, what the hell are you doing? I had nothing inside my bra except what is supposed to be there, but I had to stand and take it. I had to convince myself I was not bothered because I knew my precious visit with Nick was at stake. If I had protested, she would have refused to let me in, and that would have been that. So, I gritted my teeth and took the abuse without protest. I had flown thousands of miles to be here and nothing would prevent me from seeing my brother. I had no choice.

I stared at the prison guard and thought, "You are disgusting." I don't think it was a sexual thing, it was all about power. She was trying to intimidate me because she knew I couldn't say or do anything in return. I had to take the humiliation. I complained to the embassy afterwards, and they took the abuse very seriously. Whatever was said behind the scenes, it never happened again.

On the last day of my first trip over to India, I went to see Nick one more time before returning home. As I was leaving at the end of the visit, Nick spotted something going on nearby. He suddenly said, "Don't look." So, obviously, I looked.

Four guards in a neighbouring room were all hitting this one man. The inmate was on his knees. One guard was pulling on his hair to keep him upright, and the other three were beating him with long sticks. It was horrendous. I had never seen anything like it before. He was helpless and made no sound at all. He just had to take the beating.

The guards noticed me watching and immediately stopped. I held my breath. I didn't move. What I had seen horrified me, but I didn't know what to do. I had no power to intervene, but should I stay or leave? If I left, was I turning my back on that man, guaranteeing they would carry on beating him? Would the guards take my departure as a signal that I condoned their actions? If I stayed, was I only going to make it worse for him? Would they be angry at being caught out and take it out on the poor man?

It was awful. Whatever I did would be wrong, and I couldn't help him. Nick told me I needed to leave right away. I went to hug him goodbye and he said, "You can't. Just go." I remember being so upset because I couldn't hug him. I didn't even have time to ask my brother if that kind of punishment was ever inflicted on him. After witnessing such cruelty, my fears for Nick only grew. It was some time before he could convince me that the lads had never been the victims of mistreatment of that kind. It seemed that the Indian jailers only beat Indian inmates. Maybe it was easier to cover up.

I was left feeling traumatised by the sight of that helpless man getting beaten over and over again. It was a nightmare. I didn't want to be there, and I had done nothing wrong. I will never be able to un-see that.

As I left the prison that day, I vowed once again to do everything necessary to get Nick home, no matter what it took.

My determination to help Nick pushed me into a major decision. I thought it would be a really good idea to do the Great North Run to raise awareness of the Chennai Six. I don't know what I was thinking. I could barely run a bath. At school, I was never interested in sport, and my cross-country runs were more like leisurely walks.

The original idea was for me, our Paul and Nick to run it together when Nick finally came home. We even secured a place for Nick, but we had to defer it because he was still in prison. As the years went by, we kept on having to defer his slot time and again. The rules stated we were only supposed to take one deferment before losing the place altogether, but the organisers understood the reasons, and they kept Nick's place open until he returned.

When I said I was going to run a half marathon, my family looked at me as if I had dropped off a tree. They reckoned there was no way I could do it – and they weren't the only ones thinking along those lines. My friend Katrina was so worried about me she genuinely thought I was going to die, which said a lot about my lack of fitness.

I wasn't a healthy eater at the best of times, or even an adventurous one. I ate pasta, sausage and mash, fish fingers, and beans on toast and that was about it – although I had lost all my appetite altogether after Nick was arrested. I was small anyway, so my natural weight was only seven stones, and I lost a stone of that due to the stress, so I went down to under six stone.

The first time I tied a pair of trainers to my feet, I couldn't even run a mile. I trained on my own because I was so bad, and I didn't want to slow down other people. But, very gradually, I started to improve. There was a long cut from the hospital in Ashington to North Seaton, and I would run there and gradually increase the distance. When my runs reached four or five miles, I would head along Pegswood Straight. I felt safe running on my own but self-conscious when cars drove past. I wore a T-shirt emblazoned with the words "Help Nick Home". When drivers spotted this, they would often hit *their horn in support. My heart would burst with every toot. I loved it, and they encouraged me to keep going.*

I didn't have a lot of spare time and training took up even more but running had great physical and mental health benefits. There were times when I would put on my headphones and just work stuff through, and there were other times when I would put on my music not think about anything at all, which was a nice change.

That first Great North Run was absolutely hideous, but I made it through the 13.1 miles somehow. When I crossed the finishing line, I burst into tears of relief.

I decided I would keep doing the annual race again and again until Nick was home, but, in 2017, I faced a major problem. I developed plantar fasciitis in the heel and arch of my right foot, and it was extremely painful. The last thing I wanted to do was train for weeks on end in such pain and then run a half marathon. I wrote to my brother and received absolutely no sympathy. For normal people, pain was a warning they should stop what they were doing. For a Para, pain was something mental that could be overcome by sheer force of will. He wrote back and told me to strap up my painful foot. "You'll be fine," he said. "It's mind over matter." Before adding the classic, "Pain is weakness leaving your body." Obviously, I responded to that diagnosis by telling him to fuck off.

I'd had a tough year, and I lost a lot of motivation. I was really tired all the time, and I didn't think I would be able to maintain the training because it hurt so much every time I ran. I needed something extra special to propel me to the starting line. Then Nick wrote and told me, "If you run the Great North Run, I will do it too at the same time, in the prison at Chennai."

Well, I couldn't say no to that now, could I? I couldn't imagine how Nick was going to run a half marathon in that heat, but I knew my brother was certainly daft enough to give it a try. In return, I promised I would give it my best shot. Somehow, I managed to keep battling on with the training. I just pushed through the agony. I rolled iced bottles of water underneath my foot because a friend told me this would ease the pain. At work, I would kick off my shoe, put a frozen bottle of water under my bare foot, and roll it back and forth to get some relief.

On the day of the run, I was telling myself I could make it – but I had no idea how bad it was going to be. Two or three miles in, when I was truly doubting I could take another step, one of my colleagues from work came running up behind me. "Howay Lisa," he said. "How's your brother getting on?" I was worried I'd use up the last dregs of my energy just talking to the guy, but I managed to blurt out. "He's running it too, in India." I was in tears as soon as I said it.

That was enough to fire me up again. The idea that Nick was running the same distance in nearly 40C heat made me determined to finish this bloody race. Gary, a friend of Nick's, had messaged me that morning with some advice. "Just concentrate on putting one foot in front of the other and keep going. Just keep thinking, one more step!" he said. So that was exactly what I did. Little by little, step by step, I slowly clocked up the 13 miles. It was an extra special moment when I crossed the line, and very emotional. At the finish, a volunteer I knew called Gayle grabbed me and gave me a huge hug. There were more tears. She said, "Next year Nick will be running this with you." And he did too!

I'm not sure how I went from being somebody who couldn't even manage a mile to someone who managed to complete five consecutive Great North Runs. I suppose that shows what you can achieve when you are determined enough.

CHAPTER 30

THE GREAT CHENNAI RUN

During my first spell in prison, after we were arrested and before we were bailed, I lost a hell of a lot of weight. Six months of a terrible diet and no exercise had left me wasting away. I didn't fancy going through that again, so I knew I had to try to eat properly and exercise if I was going to keep myself occupied and stay sane. Physical fitness and building muscle had always been my thing. I used to spend hours every day keeping fit. If I had been a free man, I would have been off to the gym – but there was no gym in jail. Confronted with the harsh fact that my physical fitness would soon fade if I didn't do something about it, I decided I would take action. No gym? No problem. I would make one.

The idea came about when I was talking to another lad who liked to train, and we all chipped in to make it happen. We found some wood and stone slabs we could use as free weights. We even managed to pull a metal rod out of the ground, which we stuck up in the branches of a tree to make a pull-up bar.

The guards would always dismantle our makeshift gym, but every time they did, we rebuilt it again. In the end, we pleaded with them to leave our "equipment" alone. Surely, we said, they could recognise we were setting a good example to other prisoners.

They could watch us putting our time in prison to good use. The friendlier Indian inmates, and there were a few, were curious about what was going on and used to watch us go about our exercises. They'd never seen anything like these tattooed, muscle-bound men working out, particularly in the extreme heat. The guards decided we had a point, and our gym stayed intact from then on.

My sister managed to smuggle me in a pen, which hid a spy camera, so I took some pictures of our handiwork. I'd be the first to admit, it wasn't the poshest gym I'd ever seen, but it was effective, and I was pleased with our efforts. It was amazing what we could create from unpromising surroundings, and it helped to pass the time, which was half the battle in prison.

My improved level of fitness came in handy when Lisa decided to run the Great North Run once more to raise awareness of the Chennai Six. She freely admitted she was no runner – or any kind of natural athlete – so for her to commit to the run year after year, to do all that training and then complete the 13-mile course, was some achievement. Not long before the date of her latest half marathon, from Newcastle to South Shields, Lisa picked up an injury while training. She told me she didn't think she would be able to go ahead.

My reaction might have seemed a little harsh, but I was used to Para training where men continued with the selection process despite picking up all kinds of injuries. We couldn't just stop in the middle of a battle because we had strained something. I wrote to Lisa and said, "You think you've got an injury but what you've really got is a niggle. Also, you'll be running your 13 miles in perfect conditions. I'm stuck in a prison in the hottest part of India, where the temperature is nearly always 30 to 40C."

And that's when I made a decision and offered my sister an unusual bargain. I told her, "If you go ahead with the Great North Run, I will do it with you on the same day. We'll run it together, every step of the way, 5,000 miles apart."

My offer and the pep talk must have helped to inspire Lisa because she agreed to go ahead with the Great North Run. Now, of course, I had to honour my own side of the deal. Somehow, in baking heat, I had to come good on my promise and complete the Great Chennai Run.

The first step was to mark out a route. Obviously, the prison superintendent wasn't going to let me outside to run 13.1 miles around the streets of Chennai. That was never going to happen. Instead, we marked out a circular run round a track that took in an apex at the end. The whole circuit was almost 800 metres. That was not so very far, but I had to run nearly 21,000 metres. We worked out I would have to tackle 27 laps. All of a sudden, I wasn't sure I would be able to make it. What the hell had I got myself into?

I knew I couldn't just get up on the morning of the race and expect to be able to complete such a massive feat of endurance. I would have to train hard. So, every day for a couple of months, I ran laps around our makeshift track, sometimes early in the mornings and other times when the sun was at its fiercest. I knew I couldn't avoid those temperatures if I was to keep going for the entire course. I couldn't prevent the sun from rising or the day from getting hotter, so I would have to train myself to deal with it.

The Indian prisoners were fascinated by this. The sight of strange, British white guys running around a track during the hottest part of the day caused a lot of chatter. They must have thought we were mad. The training helped to improve my overall level of conditioning but, in all those attempts, I never once came close to completing 27 laps. In fact, 15 was the very best I could manage. I was 12 laps short, even at the peak of my fitness. What was I thinking when I had agreed to do this? I had managed to run a little over half the route at my very best. I knew I couldn't break my word and let down Lisa after everything I had said. I'd made my sister a promise, and I was determined to come good on it. I just wasn't sure how.

When they unlocked our cell at 6am on the morning of the run, it was already 29C. Nick Simpson ran the circuits with me and kept me going. Ray Tindall ran as well, at his own pace. Paul Towers encouraged us from the sidelines, and he timed us. He had managed to get hold of some oranges that gave us energy. We ran and ran as the sun rose and the day got hotter and hotter. It was so tough. In the back of my mind, I was wondering how I was going to almost double my personal best and finish the run. Other inmates were watching. Even the director of prisons, who was visiting that day, stopped to watch us run around, asking the lads what we were up to.

I was determined to keep going no matter what. The challenge reminded me of all those endurance tests in P Company, when the instructors would constantly urge us to dig deep. This time, I didn't have any NCOs bawling at me. But, one by one, the circuits fell away, we hit the 15 laps mark, and still we ran.

I am not sure where I got the strength from but, with two laps to go, I knew I was going to make it. Nick must have sensed I still had more to give because he just shouted, "Go for it!" And I did.

I don't know where it came from, but I got a sudden surge of energy. I practically sprinted the last two laps before I crossed our imaginary line. I'd done it! All 13 miles of the Great Chennai Run, and I felt great!

It took me one hour 44 mins to complete the 13 miles, and I reckon that was a pretty good time in those conditions. The average time for the Great North Run was two hours 12 minutes, so we were well within that timeframe. I don't know how I managed to get it done, but there was an immense feeling of triumph when it was over. Maybe my actions spurred on Lisa too. She managed to complete the Great North Run on the same day despite her injury, and fair play to her for that.

I smeared my legs with Deep Heat gel I borrowed off one of the Estonian lads, and then I chilled out for ages, bathed in satisfaction at my accomplishment. Astonishingly, I felt no pain or discomfort then, or the following day.

When the legendary race founder, and local hero, Brendan Foster heard what I had done, he told Lisa it was his favourite Great North Run story of all time. Considering he has heard a few over the years, that's not bad!

CHAPTER 31

A GLIMMER OF HOPE

The Indian authorities had painted themselves into a corner with us. The longer our stay in their prison dragged on, the more of an embarrassment we had become to them. By the autumn of 2017, we had served almost two years of our five-year sentence. Our story had been reported all over the world and was followed by millions. An appeal had been launched after our conviction in January 2016, but there was still no ruling in sight, all these many months later.

The authorities were beginning to realise that this was not a good look – but there was no easy way out. They wanted to save face while, at the same time, give the impression they didn't care whether or not they saved face.

When the lads used to talk about what needed to happen next to secure our release, I would say that it would take the death of one of us to end the ordeal for all of us. I also said, if that ever happened, we would be out of that prison so fast we'd be a blur. Some of the other guys expressed doubts but, somehow, I knew. I told them that was how it would play out and, in the end, I was proved right.

The captain of the Seaman Guard Ohio was a bit of a character. Dudnik Valentyn was Ukrainian, and sometimes he could be an attention seeker. Because of that, the Indians didn't take him seriously when he complained about feeling poorly. From day one, the captain declared that he was ill even though he looked fine to us. He went on about his poor state of health so much we likened him to the boy who cried wolf – forever trying to create alarm when there was no cause. He told anyone who'd listen he was dying, even when we were out on bail, but the prison authorities worked on the basis it was all just bluster. Then one day, he collapsed, and they realised he was ill for real. He was sent off to the hospital for tests.

Next thing we heard, he had moved out of the Ukrainian cell and had been admitted to live in the prison hospital. When I saw him again, he looked very frail and old. I felt sorry for the man. No-one had believed him when he said he was seriously ill because of his constant moaning, but now it looked like he was telling the truth, poor fella. We all had our differences along the way, but I didn't want to see any of our group fall ill or come to any grief. We were a fucked-up, dysfunctional family, but we were all in this terrible ordeal together from the beginning – and I wanted us to end it that way too.

The captain's legal team pleaded with the courts to give him permission to have regular medical treatment outside the prison at the Apollo Hospital in Chennai. The courts agreed and, as more months went by, it became clear to everyone that he might be dying. As I predicted, suddenly, the sluggish judicial system started to take notice of our case again. The death or serious illness of one of our number while we were in an Indian prison would be a serious embarrassment to the authorities. It also gave our legal team fresh impetus. By this time, Stephen Askins and Dr Thushara James were back on board dealing with issues surrounding the appeal. Thushara took up the captain's cause in the hope that it would finally produce a long-delayed ruling for all of us. Sure enough, the case soon reached the country's chief justice, Dipak Misra. He wanted to know why this sick man was still in their country, and why no judgment had been given on our appeal.

This was in November 2017, and our case was now with the highest judge in India, the head of the judiciary. He ordered the Chennai Appeal Court to make a decision. He went further, in fact. He set the local justices a deadline to rule on the appeal. After all the years waiting for a resolution, he was now telling the courts to bring him their final decision within two weeks.

Ironically, the captain's health, which had caused this escalation, gradually began to improve thanks to his treatment. He was responding to drugs, and he would go on to make a good recovery. But that didn't affect the judge's order. We would still have a final decision within a fortnight.

Monday 27 November 2017 was judgment day. On Sunday night that old rock anthem The Final Countdown blasted out of the radio, and it felt like an omen. Somehow, I knew this was actually going to happen. We were going to get a decision the next day. Because we were in prison, we weren't allowed to attend the court, so our legal team had to attend on our behalf. All we could do was wait and wait. I should have been used to that by now, but it was bloody torture.

As agreed, we phoned Dr Thushara James, our lawyer, at lunch time only to encounter more frustration. She told us no decision had been made. We waited all afternoon and still no word came through from the court. There were 40 cases on the lists that day, and guess who was scheduled to be the last? We were, of course.

The day was nearly over, and my hopes had started to fade. Would the hearing be postponed? Maybe. Had it gone against us yet again? Possibly. I was training outside in the early evening to keep myself occupied when Paul decided to ask the superintendent to ring the lawyer again one last time.

I'll never forget the moment when Paul returned. He walked up to the barred window and peered out at me. "Dunny?" he said. I stopped training and looked up. I can remember this moment like it was yesterday, and I still get emotional trying to explain how I felt when I heard his words.

"Case acquitted," he said. "It's over."

I always knew that death or, in this case, near-death would change everything for us.

"I bloody telt you!" I shouted at Paul, lapsing into Geordie slang. *I told you.* It was my way of expressing all the relief and elation that I was feeling all at once, as four years of hell finally ended with his simple words, "It's over."

I was exploding inside. I tried to pick up a weight, and I had to put it straight down again. I didn't know what to do with myself, so I went inside to the others and joined the jubilation in the room.

It was too late to let us out that day, so we had to spend one more night in prison. No-one slept. I was up and out of that cell at 6am so I could train hard and tire myself out. I had so much nervous energy, and I wanted those last hours to fly by. All of a sudden, things began to move, and quickly. The prison received a phone call to say the authorities wanted us out straight away. The embassy had been informed by our lawyer, and UK officials were beginning to arrive at the prison. Paul Towers went to see the superintendent, and he was told we would be departing at 11am. He returned to the cell and said, "Get your shit together." My knees just crumpled. I was struggling to deal with the news. This was actually happening. I was finally going home after four long years of imprisonment, bail and illegal detainment in India.

So, as ordered, we started to get our shit together. We packed everything we were taking with us. It wasn't much. For the Indians we had befriended, it was like Christmas, because they got everything we left behind, like tins of food and bottles of shampoo.

On the way out, our jailer told me, "I had no problems with you." That wasn't strictly true, but we were better behaved than a lot of the inmates.

The doors of the prison swung open, and we walked out of there. The embassy vehicles were waiting for us, parked at the door. The Deputy High Commissioner, Bharat Joshi, was there to shake our hands and tell us our nightmare was finally over, then the consular staff took us away and off to the hotel. We were finally free.

CHAPTER 32

LISA'S STORY: ACQUITTAL

I would have fought the whole five years to get Nick released and his verdict overturned. I swore I would do everything I could to bring my brother home. Our UK lawyer, Stephen Askins, carried on liaising with lawyers in India, and he sent us regular updates on the case, but I tried not to bombard him because he was working for free. Stephen was brilliant. I liked him a lot and really respected him, but I didn't want to take advantage of his generosity.

It was Stephen who first heard the news about the captain's poor health. When this was first mentioned I couldn't see through the implications. I didn't realise this development could lead to Nick walking free. Slowly, slowly, I began to see the bigger picture and the politics at play. It was terrible that the lads were relying on one unfortunate man's failing health to secure a release that should have come an easier way. I was talking to Stephen about what the news meant, and he said, "This is going to go back to the court. We need to get the captain back to his family."

I asked, "Can we not just get him home on compassionate grounds? Is there nothing that can be done for him?" That was exactly what our lawyers were trying to do. They were compiling an argument to set before the appeal court and, at the same time, attempting to ensure that the case of the 34 other men that had been affected by the original verdict was also placed before the highest legal official in the country. That was when there was a burst of activity. The judge ordered the case against all the men, not just the captain, should be reviewed by the appeal court within days and judges should finally come to a decision.

That was a shock. Suddenly, from nothing, it felt like we were caught in a massive whirlwind. We were so used to this case moving slowly, often at a snail's pace. Every development seemed to come with a fortnight's notice, but this was happening now, in real time. We had waited months for a major break-through like this, fearing it would take ages. Now things were moving incredibly fast. Nick had been in prison for almost two years of his five-year sentence, and we had been gifted a major opportunity to force the issue of his innocence. We could only hope that it would actually come to something, although our bitter experiences had taught us not to get carried away. I was terrified. I knew that this was our very last chance. This was the end of the legal journey. We couldn't take the case any higher. This meant everything.

On the day of the verdict, we all waited for a call or a text from Stephen. The family were gathered at Auntie Carol and Uncle Nigel's house, along with some of the reporters we knew. Like us, they were hoping for the best but fearing the worst. The waiting was awful, the tension unbelievable.

Finally, after what seemed like an endless wait, my phone bleeped into life. It was a message from Stephen. He had heard the verdict. Sending us a text was the quickest way to send the news to all the families at the same time. I hardly dared to look at the screen, but I knew I had to. Stephen's text contained only two words.

"Full acquittal."

I stared at those two little words while I digested their meaning. I could barely take it all in. Then I realised the moment we had been waiting four years for was finally here. At last, it was over! Nick was a free man and he was coming home!

We were all euphoric – and still somehow disbelieving too. It didn't seem entirely real. Mam started crying, but this time they were happy tears. We had kept a bottle of Champagne in the house for years, pledging to crack it open only to celebrate Nick's release. This magic moment seemed like a very good time to pop the cork.

Despite everything, I still had reservations. Was it really over, or were the Indian authorities lying again? Would they pull a fast one and try to drag this out even longer, perhaps with an appeal against this decision? Would they, even now, find a way to prevent Nick from leaving the country? I decided that I needed to go out to India, to see Nick and bring him back home. This wasn't over until he planted his feet on the ground at Newcastle airport.

CHAPTER 33

HOMECOMING

LISA & NICK'S STORIES

Even though we were free men, the authorities in Chennai couldn't resist the opportunity to muck us around one last time. Any hopes we had that we would be out of the country within hours were dashed by delays to our paperwork, with the court taking a couple of days to write up the proceedings. We ended up spending six more days in India waiting for the exit visas that would allow us to book flights. Some of the lads became angry and restless, and it was plainly frustrating, but we knew this would happen. India couldn't resist one last taunt. At least we were out of the prison and we knew we would go home eventually.

During the long wait, I was able to experience the luxury of staying in a hotel again. By luxury, I mean the simple ability to have a shower instead of using a bucket of water and hosepipe. I will never take running water for granted again, or the opportunity to have a room to myself. It was bliss.

I had checked into the Radisson Blu, which was next to the consulate. Staff at the Mission To Seafarers charity paid for my hotel and my flight home. They were a huge support to all of us from day one, and I'll never forget them. They helped our families and treated us like seafarers even though we weren't technically merchant seamen. They were absolutely fantastic.

There was more good news. My sister Lisa was on her way to see me and The Sun newspaper paid for her hotel. A reporter and photographer from the paper were there to report the story of our reunion and take pictures. Lisa landed very early in the morning. I rushed down to the lobby in my dressing gown to greet her, and it was very emotional. It was fantastic to see her, knowing that this whole nightmare would soon be over.

Lisa was amazing. She always stood by me. She never gave up campaigning for my release, and now I was finally free. There were some big hugs in the hotel lobby when she arrived while the photographer snapped away. We were all emotionally drained by the time we went for breakfast.

Lisa had to fly back home while I waited for all my documentation to come through. When it was all rubber-stamped and official, the Mission To Seafarers booked Paul, Ray, Nick and me onto an Emirates flight to Dubai where I would change for another flight to Newcastle.

The charity told the airline about me and what I'd been through, so the plane was set up for my journey home. I even had my own "trolley dolly" to bring drinks and look after me. I felt like I was in first class because Emirates treated me so well. It was amazing after the conditions I had been used to.

When the plane left the ground, I was worried I might make a fool of myself by bursting into tears, with the people sitting near to me wondering what on earth was wrong with this grown man who was blubbing next to them. Thankfully, I managed to avoid that embarrassment. All I felt was an incredible sense of relief that we were finally in the air. We were leaving India at last and, trust me, I was never going back there. Ever. I lost a part of my soul in that country.

The Chennai to Dubai flight was four hours. At the airport I said goodbye to Paul and Ray for the last time, as they were heading for a Manchester flight. That was quite a moment. While we couldn't wait to get home, we took time to recognise what we had been through. We had spent four years together in the worst kind of conditions. That will be a bond we will always share.

I had another long wait in Dubai. My flight wasn't due for six hours. By this stage I was completely exhausted, but I didn't dare go to sleep because there was no way I was going to miss that flight home. I'd been dreaming of this for four years, and soon it would finally be happening.

* * *

I booked my flight to India on the night of Nick's acquittal, and at 8.30 in the morning I flew out to get him. It was wonderful to meet him in the lobby of the hotel instead of having to endure another prison visit. My brother was finally out of jail and back in the real world. I really started to believe that he might actually be coming home.

Ideally, I would have flown back with Nick, but I had to return to the UK a day early because of the delays in his visa documentation. For one last time, we cursed the fact that everything took forever in India. He was planning to take a seat on the next flight back, exactly 24 hours after mine, but I was still apprehensive. I stayed in that state right up until the moment I received word that the visa problem had been sorted. When I left Nick, he had said he would come and say goodbye to me at the airport, but he was still stuck at the immigration office waiting to get his passport stamped – another long delay, even with embassy officials trying to push things along.

Nick said, "Lisa, I am going to get on that plane even if I have to sit on the wing." Even for a paratrooper that seemed excessive.

But I couldn't stop worrying. What if he didn't get back? What if he wasn't going to follow me home tomorrow? He could be stuck in India for ages. I told him, "You need to send me a picture of your passport with the visa stamped as soon as you get it so I know it will all be OK." I would continue to fret until I saw the proof.

I was at the airport waiting to fly home when that precious photo finally arrived on my phone. I could see with my own eyes that Nick had the all-important stamp in his passport. I broke down in tears. He had passed the final hurdle. This was really happening. Nick was coming home.

I flew back and began preparations for his arrival. True to her word, radio reporter Charlotte Elmore hopped over from her new job in Manchester to witness Nick's return. She even drove me to the airport in a Metro Radio car. I was planning to drive there myself, but she told me not to be so daft. She knew I would be in bits. She was right. Paul got mam ready and we picked her up. She was just grinning from ear to ear because she knew her son was on his way.

* * *

My fellow passengers knew who I was, but they left me alone with my thoughts. For years, I had dreamed of one day hearing the magical words from the captain at the end of that flight.

"We will shortly be landing in Newcastle. Please fasten your seat belts."

And then we were down, the wheels touching the tarmac. I was the last to leave the plane. The captain shook my hand and said, "Welcome home." When I reached the open door, I stood at the top of the steps and breathed deeply on the crisp, north east air. It was the freshest, sweetest mouthful I'd ever tasted.

I was led through security and my bag was already there waiting for me. Someone had taken the trouble to find it and remove it from the plane. I was treated like a VIP. It was an amazing feeling. I was walking towards the final set of doors to the outside world when suddenly I froze. I knew everybody would be waiting for me beyond those doors, and I was momentarily overwhelmed. I tried to compose myself. But I wasn't in a daze for too long because another passenger passed me and opened the door. I caught a glimpse of everyone waiting. I could even hear my dad's voice as he called, "He's there!" That shout seemed to snap me out of my head, and I bounced through those doors back to my family.

The first person to greet me was, of course, Lisa, and I gave my wonderful sister a big hug. Next, I went to my mam, who was sitting in her wheelchair. I bent low to embrace her. She hugged me back and just cried with relief. It was so wonderful to be back home with my mam. That was the best Christmas present I could have wished for.

Everyone who welcomed me at the airport had played their part in getting me home. The media were great and didn't intrude. They let me have some precious moments with my family before I went to speak to them all.

* * *

We expected to see a few media people, but the airport was packed. BBC Radio Newcastle and the Chronicle both did live streams of Nick's arrival because so many people in the north east had been following his story. Thank God his plane was on time. The airport staff were excellent, and they kept us informed about the flight's progress. They even asked us if the media were being too intrusive, and if we would like Nick to come out through a side door. I said no. After all the help and support the media had given us, it was only right for them to witness the happy ending of Nick's homecoming.

We were told, "He's landed!" There was a wait of about 20 minutes that felt like forever. Nick was last off the plane, but they processed him quickly through security. Even the ground staff were cheering and applauding. Dad was the first person to spot him. I was very emotional even though I had seen him just 24 hours earlier. This was the moment we had all been waiting and fighting for. Nick emerged into a cheering crowd, and he gave me a huge hug. I couldn't believe we had finally got him back in Newcastle, and no-one was going to be able to take my brother away from us again.

* * *

When we left the airport the first thing that hit me was the cold. Four years in one of the hottest spots in the world had absolutely ruined me for Newcastle. I was freezing!

We climbed into the car and there was a lovely final touch for the journey home – a motorcycle escort from the XXXX Crew MC Northumberland. They were all from Blyth and had supported us from the beginning. Now they escorted us all the way home, pulling out ahead of us and blocking every roundabout. We went from the airport to my mam's house without stopping once, apart from the occasional red light. It was a lovely touch.

At home my dog Cassie went crazy when she saw me. That dog had never forgotten me. It was like one of those videos you see of US soldiers coming home from Afghanistan, with the dog in a frenzy of excitement. My first food back in Britain was nice and simple. I had a McDonald's for my dinner but washed down with Champagne.

* * *

It took a while after Nick came home for us to realise that we all had our lives back. There would be no more stress or worry and no need to campaign all of the time to get him released. For a fortnight or so afterwards there were still lots of media requests. We went on Sky News with Kay Burley, Radio Two with Jeremy Vine, and I made a return visit to Victoria Derbyshire's show, but it was much better to do that interview with Nick sitting beside me.

Once the media all had their opportunity to interview Nick about his release and ask me how it felt to have my baby brother home, our lives gradually started to get back to something resembling normal.

There is one last part of our story to tell, though. When Nick came back from India, he returned to find that he had a whole new family.

We always knew Mandy and Gary existed. They were dad's children from his first marriage. They are older than us – Mandy is 51 and Gary, 49. We last saw them when Nick was just a baby, but I still had vivid childhood memories of them. Things happened in the meantime, and it does upset me to think we were estranged for so long, but back in those days it was easier for families to drift apart. They moved away to the north west with their mother, and we didn't see each other any more.

Mandy had gone on to have twins, Jade and Scott. Those twins grew up and are 28 now. I always believed that, at some point, I would search for them on social media, but I didn't realise Mandy had moved back to the north east where she lived with her husband Davy. We didn't know they were living just around the corner in Ashington. It turned out they thought we had all moved up to Scotland because my dad had worked there for a while.

I had set up the "Help Nick Home" Facebook page which used to receive a lot of messages. One night, I was sitting at home with my mam, and I read one at random. It was from a Mandy Guthrie. She was using her married name, so I didn't click. She started asking questions about my dad, and I was answering them, totally oblivious to who she really was. I thought she must have known my dad somehow, but I didn't press her. Then she sent me a private message which said, "I think I am your sister."

Oh my God.

I told mam straight away and she was very excited. We told dad, and I could tell he was over the moon too, even though he was always poker faced and didn't often show his emotions. We contacted Mandy and Gary straight away so we could meet up. Since that reunion, we have never looked back.

Nick was overwhelmed to return to the UK anyway, but when we introduced him to Mandy and Gary, and said, "Nick, this is your sister and brother," that made the reunion even more special for him. Nick came home to a bigger family than the one he had left behind.

Gary lived in York but moved to Ashington after the reunion. Gary, Nick and Paul are very similar, facially. We could tell they were all brothers and my

*dad's sons. The first Father's Day after Nick came home, we all got together –
Mandy, Gary, Nick, Paul and I – and we had a group photograph taken.*

*We gave the framed picture to my dad. It's amazing to think in the worst of
times, we were in the depths of despair because my mam was so ill and Nick
seemed lost to us, and we really felt as if there was no hope and happiness at
all in our lives, then, all of a sudden, my dad ended up getting his whole family
back together, and Nick, Paul and I got a new brother and sister. Something
positive had come from all this sadness, and for that I am eternally grateful.*

CHAPTER 34

WHAT NOW?

Everyone wanted to know what I was going to do once I was free, as if I had some big plan in mind. I'd just tell them I was going to take each day as it came. I've been told I deserve compensation from the Indian government – repayment for the four years the country had stolen from me – but that seemed not just remote, but impossible. The Indian government wouldn't want to know and, if I did take them to court, the judicial authorities would ensure the case moved at a snail's pace once again. I would be stuck inside their corrupt legal system for the second time with little chance of a favourable ruling. No, I wasn't not going to waste my time. Instead, I was looking to the future, one day at a time.

I have a job now. I want to stay in security but, unsurprisingly, I am less keen to work abroad. I did fly out for my mate Gary Hull's wedding. I'd been determined to make that special trip from the moment he had sent me that invitation in jail. I am so glad I went, even though I struggled with the idea of leaving the country. Right now, I feel like I never want to leave Britain again. For now, I'm happy being home with my mam, my dad, my brothers and sisters.

I came home to nothing. All I received from the British government on my return was an email. Even my CRB check (Criminal

Records Bureau) highlighted weapons offences. I had to ask Ian Lavery, our MP, to help me put in an appeal to the police to have the offences removed, and then liaise with the Security Industry Authority, the government body responsible for my security licence, to clear my name. A former Para offered me the chance to take his course to update my skills. After four years away, my techniques and drills had diminished, so I was grateful for that opportunity. I went up to Scotland and completed a close protection and medical course, and I started working again.

I've worked security on the London Marathon and, ironically, that involved working in the Foreign Office's own back garden. It's been an easy life after everything I have been through. I hope this book helps people become more aware of who I am and, who knows, maybe that will open some doors for me too.

The military veterans who were arrested together back in 2013 will always be known as the Chennai Six because we were all in it together, but I can't pretend to know the full stories of the other five men who shared my fate in prison. What we went through affected us all greatly, but it hurt each one of us in a different way, and I couldn't possibly guess their innermost thoughts, so I am not going to try. We each had different ways of handling our situation. This has been my story and mine alone.

From my ordeal in India, I have learned that if the chips are really down, it is still possible to move on. You can rise from adversity, no matter how terrible things may appear. Sometimes, you are in a bad place, but you can become a better, stronger person, although you do need support, and I was very fortunate to have a loving family like mine.

I owe a huge debt of thanks to Lisa for never giving up on me all the while I was trapped in India. She had to deal with both my mam's health and my imprisonment at the same time. I am very lucky, I know I am, because Lisa made sure she screamed from the highest mountain to get her brother out of jail. My sister worked with the media, and she managed to get people to sit up and take notice. She made them realise there was a massive injustice happening thousands of miles from home, but it involved a bunch of ordinary guys from the UK. Lisa made people see that this could happen to anyone, and that, if they were ever caught up in a similar situation, the British government wouldn't wave a magic wand and pull them out of the shit because that is not how the world worked.

Since I left Chennai, I am more assertive than I was. I can talk about what happened. I have had mental health problems as a direct result of my imprisonment, and I need to talk about that because I want to prevent others going down the same slippery slope. Whenever I had suicidal thoughts in Chennai, I told myself I had to man up and get on with it. I know that's an old-fashioned approach and not for everyone, but it served me well while I was banged up and could do nothing about my situation.

All the while I was stuck in Chennai, I kept telling myself to be strong and not dwell on the negative too much. I thought this was the way to battle through and out the other side. I still think that was the right strategy at the time. I have a get-on-with-it view to tackling problems that are thrown at me. Part of that comes from Para training where we had to appraise, adapt and overcome situations that we confronted. That attitude was also necessary because

I didn't want to slide into a spiral of negativity that I couldn't reverse. I knew that if I started to feel sorry for myself and dwelt on the bad things for too long, I would have ended up in a really dark place from where there might have been no escape. That was why I was determined to stay positive for as much of my time as possible, and I am sure that it helped.

The problems came later, when I was free and trying to put the bad times behind me. When I came home, the impact of everything I had been through finally hit me like a tonne of bricks. That was hard, and I know I will be dealing with the fall-out for the rest of my life.

Like all Paras, I pride myself on being more resilient than most, but even I had days when I was in absolute despair. I didn't want to show it though, not to anyone. Instead, I would hide myself away. That wasn't easy in a jail full of hundreds of people. I would go to the one place I knew I'd be undisturbed by anybody − behind the prison toilets. It wasn't the most pleasant place to sit and think, but at least I knew I could be on my own. This unlikely location was where I went for some peace, and when I wanted to speak to God to ask him why this was happening to us. Why did we deserve it? What was the reasoning behind us all being banged up in prison like this with no end in sight?

I think I am getting better at controlling my emotions, but I know that it is never going to be easy. I've been through far too much. When I was younger, if I got angry, I used to punch the door or the walls, and guess what? The wall didn't get hurt, I did. It took me a while to work out that there was no point to any of that. The wall had no feelings.

When I joined the Paras, I was programmed to switch off my emotions because I had orders to follow and a job to do. I used to bottle everything up. But I'm not in the military and I don't do that now. I could go back to being that steely man again, but I doubt it would do me any good. Would I be a nicer person if I was the same way in civilian life as I had been in the army? Probably not.

I am not the same man I was before my ordeal in Chennai. I haven't got the same concentration levels I once had. Some days I don't know where the hours have gone. My brother Paul once watched me go into one room and come out again, then go into another for no reason. He said, "You don't look as if you know what you are doing. You look lost." And he was right. At that moment, I didn't know what I was doing, and I am convinced those lapses of concentration are a side-effect of what I went through in India.

The good news is that generally I'm doing OK. I have my bad days, but I will never stop appreciating being home with my friends and my family, and I am looking forward to the future with hope. I'm not a particularly spiritual or religious man, but I would say that I had to go to a very dark place in order to see the light again. Some people go to that dark place and stay there. There were times during our imprisonment when I was in despair, reduced to tears, and I doubted that I would ever get home again, but no matter how low I felt, I never gave up, and I am proud of that fact.

I'm Nick Dunn. I kept going, I did not buckle, and I made it home.

TIMELINE

- **October 12, 2013** – MV Seaman Guard Ohio is brought into the port of Tuticorin by the coastguard.
- **October 18, 2013** – 10 crew and 25 guards on board the MV Seaman Guard Ohio arrested. Nick is 27 years old.
- Placed in Palayamkottai Central prison in Tirunelveli.
- **October 23, 2013** – after 11 days, 22 of the 23 foreign nationals were transferred to Puzhal Central prison in Chennai.
- **December 2013** – bail granted then revoked.
- **February 2014** – the 2,158-page charge sheet is given to all defendants.
- **March 2014** – a 136,000-signature petition is delivered to the British government seeking prime minister's help to get bail.
- **March 26, 2014** – bail granted to 33 of the 35 accused after six months in prison.
- **July 2014** – Madras High Court throws out the charges.
- **October 2014** – Q Branch of the police launches an appeal against this verdict.
- **July 2015** – Indian Supreme Court overturns High Court verdict and orders a trial.

- **January 11, 2016** – Judge sentences the accused men to five years in prison. The appeal process begins.
- **November 27, 2017** – Chennai appeal court acquits the men because they had the necessary papers for the guns and were not technically inside Indian territorial waters.
- The Chennai Six endured a total of **four years and one month** held in India, either in prison, on bail or technically free but not allowed to leave the country. No crimes had even been committed.
- **7 December 2017** – Nick Dunn finally returns home to his family in the UK.

NICK'S ACKNOWLEDGEMENTS

I dedicate this book to my amazing sister, Lisa Dunn. She always knew I was innocent and put her life on hold to fight for justice for me. Lisa is an inspirational woman who worked tirelessly on my behalf for four years until I was finally freed. I am forever in her debt.

Lisa shares that dedication with my mam, Margaret Dunn, who showed huge grit and determination and did not succumb to a double aneurysm. My mam always believed she would see her son again, and she gave me the strength to carry on till the finish line.

I would like to say a huge thank you to the Manchester branch of the Parachute Regimental Association for their true, airborne support, and for making Lisa and me honorary members.

The financial assistance I received from the Army Benevolent Fund, the Royal British Legion and the Parachute Regiment helped to keep a roof over my head during the time I was in India, and I am extremely grateful for that. The Mission To Seafarers also did a fantastic job helping all of the families financially.

My great mate, Gary Hull, deserves a special mention for his unflagging support and those much-appreciated food parcels.

Thank you to my local MP, Ian Lavery, for raising awareness of our ordeal in Parliament, and thanks also to all the local, north east media which got behind us from the beginning and showed everybody that we were innocent.

My legal team, and Dr Thushara James in particular, earned my gratitude. Thushara was the best lawyer we could possibly have had to help us win our appeal. Stephen Askins deserves a special mention. Our amazing UK lawyer worked for nothing for years to get us freed. I can never thank him enough.

Ray Tindall and Paul Towers get a massive thank-you from me for the way they built up the defence case for our lawyers until we were finally proven innocent of all charges.

Thanks to Jordan Wylie for raising awareness in the UK and even coming all the way out to Chennai and doing a 10K run there to raise awareness of the Chennai Six.

Thank you to everyone at the British Consul in Chennai, including Bharat Joshi, Petula James and, in particular, Sharon D'Sylva and Manisha Hariharan for everything that you did for us.

I must say a big thank-you for all the support I received from the people in my home town of Ashington, Northumberland, and the rest of the UK.

I would like to thank Mirror Books for giving me this opportunity to tell my full story for the first time. Special thanks to executive editor, Jo Sollis, for believing in this book, editor Giles Broadbent for all his hard work on it, and communications executive Melanie Sambles.

A big thank-you goes to best-selling author Damien Lewis. Without him, this book would not have happened. He put me in touch with my fantastic literary agent, Phil Patterson, who worked so hard to get this book published. Thanks also to my ghostwriter, Howard Linskey, for always believing that my story should be told and for spending so many hours helping me to put it on the page.

LISA'S ACKNOWLEDGEMENTS

I would firstly like to thank my wonderful dad for being my absolute rock through this. He also suffered greatly throughout this ordeal but gave so much strength and support to Nick and me.

I would like to say a huge thank you to my very close friends, who could not have been more supportive. Very special thanks to Alan Stanfield, Jill Kalogerou, Kate Rickard, Katrina Ross and Stacey Johnson. I'll always be eternally grateful.

The campaign to free Nick was a long and difficult one, and Nick and I have many people to thank for his eventual release. There are too many extremely kind people and organisations to be able to thank individually, but the following all played a part in supporting me and Nick.

- *Stephen Askins*
- *Dr Thushara James*
- *Ian Lavery MP and staff*
- *Former MEP Jonathan Arnott and staff*
- *The MPs of the British men detained*
- *Malcolm Aitken*
- *Mission To Seafarers staff, with special thanks to the Rev Ken Peters and Ben Bailey*
- *The International Transport Federation*
- *Human Rights at Sea*
- *Professor James Tooley*

- *Dr Barrie Craven*
- *Jordan Wylie*
- *Ashington Rugby Club*
- *Badlanders Motorcycle Club*
- *Red & White MC Northumberland (formerly XXXX Crew MC Northumberland)*
- *Phil Campion*
- *Propeller Club Liverpool & London*
- *Standby Productions*
- *Whittaker & Co*
- *Global Maritime Recruitment Solutions*
- *SCEG (Security in Complex Environments Group)*
- *Charlie Lawson*
- *John Bowe*
- *Lee Dargue*
- *Stuart Paver*
- *Sarah Blackman*
- *London International Shipping Week 2017*
- *The Great Run Company*
- *The Royal British Legion*
- *The Parachute Regiment Association*
- *Pegasus Appreciation Group, especially Rich Greasley and Lee Crichton*
- *Justice for Cpl Stewart McLaughlin Campaign*
- *Captain Richard Phillips*
- *Colin Eastaway*
- *David McMullen*
- *James Wadley*

- *The British Embassy staff in London, particularly the desk officers Jo-Ann Sibbons, Shahda Ghufoor, Kerry Morris and Gary Fisher*
- *Prisoners Abroad*
- *Lindsay, Alan, Sally and Alice Bell*
- *Friends and colleagues at Northumbria Police with special thanks to Susan Taylor with whom I travelled to and from work. For more than four years, and then many more months after Nick came home, the 19-mile journey was dominated by me sounding off to Susan. I would like to thank her for listening and being such a good support.*
- *All the media who highlighted the case and supported the campaign And finally, every single person throughout Ashington, the north east, the UK and worldwide who supported our family and the campaign, everybody who donated funds, and to every person who showed their support with our campaign on social media*

Howard Linskey

Howard Linskey is the best-selling author of 10 novels. His books have been published in the UK, Germany, the Czech Republic, Australia, New Zealand and the USA. He is a former journalist from the north east of England and now lives with his wife and daughter in Hertfordshire.